Challenging Learning

Challenging Learning offers advice and techniques for helping children of all ages develop into confident, thoughtful and independent learners. Based around the acronym ASK (attitudes, skills and knowledge), this essential guide explores attitudes, skills and knowledge to learning. It considers the strategies that can help teachers to challenge their pupils to think more skilfully and logically and how to develop these techniques more effectively.

Drawing on the latest research from some of the most respected experts in the field, *Challenging Learning* encourages independent thinking and a spirit of inquiry in pupils of all ages. Through the use of rich examples of classroom interactions, this book offers strategies that will help pupils to produce their own thoughtful conclusions, develop their own concepts, examine logic and remain open to alternatives.

Highlights include:

- effective teaching strategies including FACTS, the Teaching Target model and the Learning Pit model;
- up-to-date research and theory from leading experts;
- practical suggestions and principles to help you design and develop your own lessons.

For everyone living or working with children – particularly teachers, parents, carers and youth workers – this book shows some of the best ways to enhance children's learning, including how to question, praise, give feedback and encourage more effectively.

James Nottingham is a leader in transforming up-to-date research into best practice for teaching and learning. Initially a teacher and leader in schools for 3–18 year olds, he now runs his own company, Challenging Learning, with a team of consultants across Scandinavia, the UK and Australia.

Challenging Learning

Theory, effective practice and lesson ideas to create optimal learning in the classroom

Second edition

James Nottingham

Routledge
Taylor & Francis Group

LONDON AND NEW YORK

Second edition published 2016
by Routledge
2 Park Square, Milton Park, Abingdon, Oxon OX14 4RN

and by Routledge
711 Third Avenue, New York, NY 10017

Routledge is an imprint of the Taylor & Francis Group, an informa business

First edition published by JN Publishing 2010

British Library Cataloguing in Publication Data
A catalogue record for this book is available from the British Library

Library of Congress Cataloging-in-Publication Data
Nottingham, James.
   Challenging learning: theory, effective practice and lesson ideas
   to create optimal learning in the classroom/James Nottingham.—
   Second edition.
   pages cm
   1. Effective teaching. 2. Communication in education. 3. Problem
   solving—Study and teaching. 4. Critical thinking—Study and
   teaching. I. Title.
   LB1025.3.N677 2016
   371.102—dc23
   2015016528

ISBN: 978-1-138-92304-1 (hbk)
ISBN: 978-1-138-92305-8 (pbk)
ISBN: 978-1-315-68537-3 (ebk)

Typeset in Bembo and Helvetica Neue
by Florence Production Ltd, Stoodleigh, Devon, UK

For Jill, Ava, Harry, and Phoebe
My family, my world

'Sixty years ago I knew everything; now I know nothing;
education is a progressive discovery of our own ignorance.'
(Will Durant, 1885–1981)

Contents

Foreword

This valuable book encourages teachers to challenge their pupils to think more deeply, skilfully and logically through carefully structured classroom dialogue. It also tells them how to do it.

Drawing on a substantial body of research and theory by Carol Dweck, John Hattie, Matthew Lipman and many others, James Nottingham concludes that pupils who have not been taught to think and solve problems tend to believe that inborn aptitude determines their levels of achievement in school and life. As a result, they do not respond positively to challenges and their performance often remains low. On the other hand, students who are treated as if they are intelligent, actually become more so if they are used to being challenged and supported through their struggles. If, for example, they are taught demanding content and are expected to defend their answers, to explain their rationales and to make connections to other content, they learn more, and learn more quickly. They become more conscious of their own thinking and are able to take control of it. They develop a positive, efficacious self-image and tend to think of themselves as continual and powerful learners.

Through the use of rich examples of classroom interactions, James shows teachers how to stretch children's minds more by pressing them to provide evidence, to test the logic of their ideas and to give a rationale for their explanations rather than just accepting and praising 'right' answers. These strategies will help children to produce their own thoughtful conclusions, develop their own concepts, examine logic and remain open to alternatives.

If more teachers were to use the interactive classroom strategies suggested by James Nottingham in this book, then their pupils would surely grow into more careful thinkers, teachers would gain greater skill in conducting their classroom dialogues and, who knows, the world might even become a more thoughtful place.

Arthur L Costa, Ed.D.
Professor Emeritus, California State University, Sacramento
Author of *Habits of Mind*

Author's welcome

I wrote the first edition of *Challenging Learning* in 2010. Since then it has been translated into four languages, and become a bestseller in Denmark and Sweden. This second edition has been updated and improved in line with ever more current theory and practice.

The aim of *Challenging Learning* is to provide you with many practical suggestions to make your work with pupils more enjoyable and effective. I've also included principles to help you design your own lessons based on some of the most up-to-date and impressive research on teaching and learning.

The book contains lesson ideas (Chapter 8) and an explanation of the Learning Pit that is the foundation of the book. Both of these sections are preceded by five 'FACTS' of effective learning and teaching, covering:

F eedback

A pplication

C hallenge

T hinking

S elf-esteem

Taken together, FACTS, the Teaching Target and the Learning Pit models, and the lesson ideas represent much of my work over the last 20 years. I hope you find them useful and are inspired to try out some of the strategies and ideas with your own pupils.

James Nottingham
March 2015
www.challenginglearning.com
www.jamesnottingham.co.uk

Preface

'The only time my education was interrupted was while I was at school.'
(Winston Churchill, 1874–1965)

I began learning the moment I left school. Before then, I had been bored by a pre-packaged curriculum and by information transmitted by teachers who did not inspire me.

And yet, after an eventful 3 years working variously in the chemical industry, as a charity worker in apartheid South Africa and then as a child care officer in a school for deaf children, I decided to apply for teacher training, convincing myself I could put information across in a more interesting and entertaining way than those who had taught me. What, or rather who, I found at teacher training college, however, turned my ideas about education upside down. Chris Rowley, a lecturer at the then Charlotte Mason College in Ambleside, Cumbria, challenged us, provoked us and confused us.

At the beginning of our first 'lecture', Chris pointed to Wansfell, the mountain behind the lecture room. He asked us to climb to the top and work out where we were. End of lesson 1. Lesson 2 began with: 'Well, what did you find out?' I thought this was a very simple question. 'We were sat at the top of Wansfell in the middle of the Lake District National Park', I stated with not a moment's hesitation. Others said similar things.

'What else can you tell me?' inquired Chris. Someone said, 'We were on a mountain'. Others said: 'we were sat on a hill looking over a northern town'. Others suggested we were in a beautiful part of the world. Chris then questioned our use of particular words: 'Is it a mountain or a hill?' Some of us said 'hill', others said 'mountain', one or two wondered what the difference was and some even wanted to know what difference it made.

'Is it a northern town or a southern town?' The Scots among us were adamant it was a southern town, despite Ambleside's usual characterisation as a north-west town.

'It's beautiful in what sense?' We thought it was because the landscape looked nice.

'Does all landscape look nice?' No, but this does with its drystone walls and roaming sheep.

'Without drystone walls and roaming sheep, is it not beautiful?'

And so this experience continued until we were all arguing about where to draw the line between northern and southern England (I still maintain the M62 is the border), whether geography determines culture, and whether the classification of a mountain in the UK as something over 1,000ft is credible given the size of mountains in other parts of the world.

Was this learning? It certainly didn't feel like it. That was until we had to write our first assignment and I realised, despite my fears to the contrary, that I had plenty to say. In fact, I still have that first assignment, so taken aback was I by Chris's response to it. As I mentioned, I didn't enjoy school for a number of reasons; one was that lessons seemed boring – copying notes placed on the overhead projector day after day was an activity that dulled rather than awakened my mind. My grades were poor and I grew up believing that I wasn't a particularly good scholar. But then Chris changed all that, bit by bit.

The grade he gave me for my first assignment was 69 per cent, 1 per cent short of a 'first'. That was surprising enough, given my lack of belief in my abilities, but it was his comments that rocked me so completely that I can still remember the feeling to this day.

> The introduction and conclusion, in themselves, are excellent and, in themselves, I find the format of lots of contrasting arguments fascinating. They reflect considerable work and much reading of New Internationalist (amongst other texts). Your choice of quotations, comments and thoughts is excellent, and had this been an article for publication in a magazine like NI I'd say it was of journalistic (no, that flatters journalists – it's better) quality.
>
> As an essay I've got a problem in deciding how to mark it. To what extent do I reward something from which you have clearly gained enormously, both in terms of IT use (note: IT was in its infancy, at least in education, in 1992) and in terms of your own thinking?
>
> The problem is, fundamentally, that as an essay it doesn't gradually develop an argument. It's too emotive; it lacks any logical thread; it doesn't credit individual facts. In short, it isn't an essay! Because you leave the reader to interpret, intuitively, so many of your contrasting arguments, which I have done but which can't be assumed, I feel that the university would give a 2:1 rather than a 1st. There remains an issue here, and I'm willing to discuss it!

Discuss it? What did he mean, 'Discuss it?' I thought teachers simply told pupils what was right and what was wrong and that was that!

Before this feedback, the only comments I'd ever received consisted of ticks, crosses, grades and the odd comment such as 'good' or 'improve your spelling'. But here, Chris was not only giving me fully developed and specific feedback but his last sentence was inviting me to negotiate the grade with him. This blew me away. Negotiate with a teacher? Hitherto, teachers had possessed an air of infallibility. Weren't they the authoritative ones that told pupils what was right and wrong?

From that moment on, I felt like a co-inquirer in a world of learning rather than a novice expecting my mind to be filled with knowledge by the teacher. I felt as if education was about thinking and good judgement rather than just learning facts presented as being unambiguous and unequivocal. I began to believe that I could become a successful learner as well as a proficient teacher.

Chris changed my entire perspective on education and learning in that first term and helped me to develop it further in my 4 years at the college. He recommended that I investigate Philosophy for Children (P4C) as a way of putting my ideals into practice in the classroom and he encouraged communities of inquiry (a group of people coming together to engage in collaborative investigation) in almost every 'lecture' we ever had with him.

Chris Rowley is one of the main reasons I achieved a first class honours degree and why I do what I do today.

Other influences

As well as Chris Rowley, I have, and therefore this book has, been greatly influenced by:

My wonderful wife, Jill, who has always challenged and encouraged me and ensured that my work is grounded in theory as well as practice.

Carol Dweck, the Lewis and Virginia Eaton Professor of Psychology, Department of Psychology at Stanford, with whom I enjoyed two conference tours in 2010 and 2014.

John Hattie, Professor of Education and Director of Melbourne Education Research Institute, with whom I have the great pleasure of working and presenting regularly.

Dr John Edwards, a master in the art of keynote speaking and professional coaching, and the first person I heard using the idea of a 'pit' (see Chapter 7). I owe him a great deal.

Furthermore, as you read through this book, you will not be surprised to learn that I have been significantly influenced by P4C. Developed by Professor Matthew Lipman in the early 1970s, P4C places inquiry and questioning at the heart of learning. For my initial interest I thank Chris Rowley, and for my continued inspiration, the many good folk of SAPERE,[1] most notably Roger Sutcliffe, Steve Williams, Sara Liptai and Will Ord (more information about P4C can be found at www.sapere.org.uk and www.p4c.com).

Ready, fire, aim!

I like this phrase. It works for me when designing a presentation, writing a book, or developing a skill. As far as I can tell, the phrase was first coined by open-source expert Clay Shirky (www.shirky.com) though Michael Fullan (www.michael fullan.ca) seems to have used it often too.

The idea is that once I find something worth doing (ready), I get on with it (fire) and assess my efforts later. Then I readjust my efforts (aim) and keep trying (fire again). This helps me to avoid the sometimes-disabling notion that I have to understand a problem fully or design an infallible solution in great detail and with great coherence before I can begin tackling it.

The maxim 'ready, fire, aim' also helps me to guard against the danger that I will invest so much effort into the initial work of understanding and designing that I will not want to face up to outcomes that seem to challenge my carefully constructed solutions. In education, it reminds us of the necessary virtues of energy, experiment, evaluation and constant adjustment.

A favourite interpretation of the maxim comes from Guy Kawasaki, one of the people responsible for the success of the Macintosh computer. He uses it to describe how he writes books:

> First, I make the slides (ready). Then I give the presentation many times (fire). Then I write the book (aim). I like to perfect the slides and presentation first and elaborate on them to write a book. If your speeches work, then your book will too. The opposite is not true.

That is exactly how I have come to write this book; within it, you will find the best ideas I have presented, had critiqued many times over and then presented again and again to educational audiences all around the world.

'Ready, fire, aim' is also a good route to follow in reading and applying the contents of this book. Don't wait around until you have digested all the theoretical parts – try some of the practical suggestions as soon you have an understanding of the overall goals of Challenging Learning.

I've systematised this in the following way if you want to give the 'ready, fire, aim' approach a go:

Ready

Read the following pages first, as these will give you an overview of what the lesson ideas are trying to achieve. These include:

- Natalie the Navigator on page 1.
- The ASK model on pages 34–42.
- The Teaching Target model on pages 53–58.
- The Learning Pit model on pages 109–126.
- The summary pages for each of the FACTS chapters on pages 29–30, 49–50, 75–76, 94–96, 107–108.
- The notes about wobblers on pages 64–65.

Fire

Have a go with the lesson plans so that you get a better feeling for the way that the concepts and principles explored in this book work in practice.

Aim

Finally, read the five FACTS chapters (Chapters 2–6) outlining the theoretical underpinning for the lesson ideas. This will help to deepen the Challenging Learning experience for you.

1

What is challenging learning?

Natalie the Navigator

A few months ago, I was with a friend driving to a theatre in a town we didn't know well. Normally, that would be okay because we would simply follow the instructions given by his GPS. We call it Natalie the Navigator, because of its beautiful female voice. This time, Natalie wasn't working. We were stranded with no idea which way to go. That sounds unremarkable until I admit this wasn't the first time we'd driven to that same theatre. In fact, we'd been there three times already in the previous 12 months. But each time, we'd relied on Natalie to get us there and in so doing had lost the ability to navigate ourselves, at least to some degree.

Natalie the Navigator
'How many students rely on their teacher to guide them, in much the same way as a driver relies on their GPS?'

This got me thinking: how many pupils in schools right now are making a similar mistake, not of course with navigation, but with their learning? How many pupils rely on their teacher to get them to the answer? How many sit back waiting for directions, knowing full well that their teacher will not only show them how to get to the destination but will even decide the starting point? Sure, when it works, like GPS, this strategy is great. But what happens when there is no Natalie, no teacher to guide them – then what? Won't these pupils be just as lost as Gordon and me?

My teaching experience in both primary and secondary schools has shown me that whenever I stop pretending to be Natalie the Navigator and act as if I were a personal trainer instead – encouraging learners, offering focused feedback and, above all, challenging them as much as possible – that is when pupils grow most. It is also when pupils learn how to learn and, in so doing, improve their self-esteem, become more self-reliant and achieve more.

Challenging Learning shows you how this can work in your classroom.

Inspiration for the title, *Challenging Learning*

The title, *Challenging Learning*, was inspired by a passage from *Thinking in Education* by Matthew Lipman,[2] a well-thumbed book in my office that is filled with highlighted passages, notes in the margins and corners that are dog-eared. I have added the italics to the last paragraph.

> It is a fact often noted that very young children begin their formal education in kindergarten as lively, curious, imaginative and inquisitive creatures. For a while, they retain these wonderful traits. But then gradually a decline sets in, and they become passive . . .
>
> Since the child's first 5 or 6 years were spent at home, and since this did not seem to impair the child's intellectual energies, it seems strange to condemn the child's background for a subsequent loss of curiosity and imagination. It is more likely due to the nature of schooling. What the child probably expects from the school is a surrogate home and a surrogate family – a surrounding that constantly stimulates thought and speech. Even when it is uncaring, as it often is, the home environment contains so much to be learned, so much to be experienced, that it represents a constant challenge to the very young child. What the child discovers at school, on the other hand, is a completely structured environment. Instead of events that flow into other events, there is now a schedule that things must conform to.
>
> Instead of statements that can be understood only by gleaning their significance from the entire context in which they occur, there is a classroom language that is uniform and rather indifferent to context and therefore fairly devoid of enigmatic intimations.
>
> The natural mysteriousness of the home and family environment is replaced by a stable, structured environment in which all is regular and explicit. Children gradually discover that such an environment is seldom an

invigorating or challenging one. Indeed, it drains them of the capital fund of initiative and inventiveness and thoughtfulness that they brought with them to school. It exploits their energies and gives them little back in return. Before long, children become aware that schooling is enervating and dispiriting rather than animating or intellectually provocative. In short, schooling provides few natural incentives to thinking in the way that the home environment does. A drop-off in pupil interest is the natural consequence.

To professionals who have worked long and hard to improve the education of all children, these remarks may be hard to take. But they are not intended as accusations. Teachers do what they have been trained to do, and by and large they do it well . . . Indeed many teachers are aware that the constant insistence upon order and discipline may be stultifying and can destroy the very spontaneity that they would most like to cultivate and cherish.

The solution lies in the establishing of conditions that will arouse and guide curiosity. We need more stories and less facts, for narrative develops an understanding of sequence; we need more dialogue and less transmission of knowledge, for it is through dialogue that we learn most; and we need more challenge and less instruction, since it is from challenge that one grows in body, mind and spirit.

This last paragraph gripped me when I first read it and has challenged me ever since. How can I use more narrative, dialogue and challenge while at the same time teach an over-stuffed curriculum and meet every demand that is placed upon me as a teacher? This book is my answer to that question. The first part of the book establishes a framework for *Challenging Learning* using the acronym FACTS to organise five essential facets of an effective education that aims towards self-reliance. The following five chapters of the book (the FACTS chapters) are dedicated to each one in turn.

FACTS: the foundations of challenging learning

Feedback

Feedback should provide information – relating to a set task or to the process of learning – that helps move pupils towards their learning objectives. 'The most powerful single modification that enhances achievement is feedback.' (John Hattie)[3]

Application

Pupils apply themselves when they pay close attention to their learning and persist in their efforts. How much they apply themselves is often a product of the value they place on the learning goal multiplied by the level of expectation they have of achieving the goal. 'Mediocrity achieves more with application than superiority does without it.' (Baltasar Gracián, 1601–1658)

Challenge

Challenge underpins all of the other factors. It involves helping people to overcome difficulties intrinsic to a task or that the teacher has set for a purpose. 'We need more challenge and less instruction, since it is from challenge that one grows in body, mind and spirit.' (Matthew Lipman)[4]

Thinking

To teach thinking is to help children develop conceptual capacities, powers of judgement and practical wisdom. 'The development of general ability for independent thinking and judgement should always be placed foremost, not the acquisition of special knowledge.' (Albert Einstein)[5]

Self-esteem

Self-esteem involves confidence, self-worth and the personal resources for working through setbacks. 'It's lack of faith that makes people afraid of meeting challenges, and I believe in myself.' (Muhammad Ali, 1942–)

FACTS: some reasons why

In his inaugural speech as Professor of Education at the University of Auckland in 1999,[6] John Hattie made the following claims based on his extensive comparative studies of educational research:

1   Achievement is enhanced to the degree that pupils and teachers set and communicate appropriate, specific and challenging goals.

2   Achievement is enhanced as a function of feedback (i.e. when feedback is increased, so is achievement).

3   Increases in pupil learning involve not only surface and deep learning but also a re-conceptualisation of information.

This goes part way to explaining why I have included feedback and challenge as two of the five key chapters in my book, and why the lesson plans at the back are concerned with concepts and re-conceptualisation.

As for focusing on thinking, self-esteem and application, these are included as a result of research during my time as director of a multi-million pound project (RAIS) to raise the aspirations of young people in north-east England.[7] Over 5 years, the RAIS project focused on the development of thinking skills and self-esteem and sought to improve the application of all learners. Recognition of the positive outcomes of this project led to it winning a prestigious award for the significant contribution it had made to the improvement of life chances of young people in north-east England.

Thus, the five aspects of FACTS identify the main theoretical underpinnings that will enhance all Challenging Learning lessons.

2 Feedback

FEEDBACK
APPLICATION
CHALLENGE
THINKING
SELF-ESTEEM

'If there's a single principle teachers need to digest about classroom feedback, it's this: The only thing that matters is what students do with it. No matter how well the feedback is designed, if students do not use the feedback to move their own learning forward, it's a waste of time.'

(Dylan Wiliam, 2014)[8]

Three questions for feedback

At the heart of feedback are three key questions:

1 What am I trying to do?
2 How much progress have I made?
3 What should I do next?

Feedback key points

Definition

Feedback should provide information relating to the task, or process, that helps move pupils towards their learning objectives.

Importance

Feedback is one of the most powerful influences on learning and achievement if it:

- relates to clear and specific goals;

- stimulates a thoughtful, proactive response on the part of the learner;

- allows for learning from mistakes, rather than fearing them or even being punished for making them.

Be wary

Be wary of giving feedback that relates to the person (e.g. 'good boy' and 'clever girl') or thinking that praise is always a positive form of feedback. Both feedback and praise should relate to performance and progress, not to the person.

What is feedback?

Feedback is a term used in many contexts. The definition adopted here is: Feedback should provide information relating to the task, or the process, that helps move pupils towards their learning objectives.

This can then be split into three categories, by considering information that helps a pupil:

1   understand the goal or learning intention;

2   know where they are in relation to the goal;

3   realise what they need to do to bridge the gap between the current position and the goal.

It is important to note that feedback may well focus on content and process (including types of thinking), and even on pupils' self-beliefs. For example, as well as identifying what needs to be understood (knowledge), feedback might also draw attention to pupils' thinking strategies (e.g. by testing their assumptions) as well as exploring their beliefs about themselves, including their levels of self-confidence about learning. As Winnie and Butler put it in 1994, 'Feedback is information with which a learner can confirm, add to, overwrite, tune, or restructure . . . whether that information is domain knowledge (content), metacognitive knowledge (thinking about performance), beliefs about self and tasks, or cognitive tactics and strategies'.[9]

When should feedback occur?

Feedback should follow the first attempt by pupils to understand, create or do something (see Figure 2.1) and should identify what needs to be done to make further progress towards a clear learning goal (remember 'ready, fire, aim!').

The feedback should also be timely enough for pupils to remember not only the decisions they made but also their reasons for making those decisions and for rejecting other alternatives. If feedback is given weeks or even days after the pupils have attempted the learning, then its effect will be weakened.

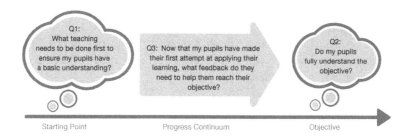

FIGURE 2.1 The three key feedback questions

Do teachers provide enough feedback?

Common sense tells us we need feedback to learn

Feedback gives us information about how we are performing in relation to an objective and what our next steps might be. In the absence of this information, it is reasonable to suppose that progress would either be limited or misdirected. We have all experienced the difficulties that arise from not knowing what is expected of us or how we are doing. This common-sense view is supported by research.

Statistical evidence identifies feedback as a key factor in learning

Statistical evidence, particularly from Lysakowski and Walberg,[10] Marzano *et al.*,[11] Black and Wiliam,[12] and Hattie[13] shows that feedback is one of the most powerful influences on learning and achievement.

> The effect of feedback on learning . . . calculated from statistical data in 54 studies containing a combined sample of 14,689 pupils in approximately 700 classes . . . suggests average percentiles on learning outcomes of between 50% and 83% improvement . . . and appeared constant from elementary level through college, and across socioeconomic levels, races, private and public schools, and community types.[14]

There isn't enough feedback in schools at present

> Carless (2006) asked pupils and teachers whether teachers provided detailed feedback that helped pupils improve their next assignments. About 70% of the teachers claimed they provided such detailed feedback often or always, but only 45% of students agreed with their teachers' claims (Hattie, 2009).[15]

Is all feedback positive?

Despite strong evidence that feedback is a crucial factor in pupil progress, not all forms of feedback are positive. For example, a number of authors have shown that simply telling pupils their answers are right or wrong (as a form of feedback) can have a negative impact on learning.

In *Assessment for Learning: Beyond the black box*, members of the Assessment Reform Group (UK) identified several aspects of feedback that did not bring gains in learning. These included:

- a tendency for teachers to assess quantity of work and presentation rather than quality of learning;
- too much attention given to marking and grading, much of it tending to lower the self-esteem of pupils, rather than providing advice for improvement;
- too much emphasis on comparing pupils with each other – a practice that demoralises the least successful learners;
- teachers' feedback to pupils too often serving social and managerial purposes rather than helping them to learn more effectively;
- teachers not knowing enough about their pupils' learning needs.[16]

Furthermore, in the seminal work of Carol Dweck,[17] as well as in the work of Black and Wiliam,[18] there is a warning about forms of feedback that draw attention to the personal attributes of pupils, rather than to their performance in relation to a set task. Such feedback can lead to an increased fear of failure and/or behaviour that seeks to minimise further risk or challenge. This is explored in more depth in the chapter on self-esteem.

What type of feedback is best?

A more detailed synthesis of 74 meta-analyses in Hattie's (1999) database . . . demonstrated that the most effective forms of feedback provide cues or reinforcement to learners; are in the form of video-, audio- or computer-assisted instructional feedback; and/or relate to goals, whereas programmed instruction, praise, punishment and extrinsic rewards were the least effective for enhancing achievement.

(Hattie and Timperley, 2007)[19]

Deciding on the best form of feedback will depend on context but using the types that follow, when appropriate, will enrich your Challenging Learning lessons. They are explored in turn throughout the rest of the chapter.

Coaching

Coaching is a form of intensive, planned encouragement and guidance targeted at developing essential skills, positive attitudes and other personal resources for life and learning.

Dialogue

Dialogue is the most immediate and collaborative way of feeding back to pupils, providing both a stimulus and a model for their own reflections on learning as well as their strategies for understanding. See pages 10–11 for more details.

Formative and summative assessment

Formative assessment is feedback that provides explanation, diagnosis, prompting and/or elaboration to pupils in response to their efforts. Formative assessment enables them to make further progress. Usually, the most complete form of feedback is dialogue. This is explored on page 14.

Praise

Although praise is often the first and perhaps most pleasant form of feedback given and received, it has some consequences that are counterproductive, particularly when pupils are praised for completing easy tasks. This problem is explored in depth in the chapter on self-esteem (see pages 97–108).

Peer and self-reviews

According to Nuthall,[20] most feedback that pupils receive on a day-to-day basis comes from their peers, and is incorrect. On pages 16–19 there are some suggestions for ways to counteract this problem.

Video and computer feedback

Although I have no data to support this claim, apart from anecdotal evidence, pupils seem to respond well to computer evaluation of their achievement and to video evidence of their performance. They feel no sense of disapproval in the computer evaluation; the video evidence is often self-explanatory. This is explored on page 28 and is something Hattie and Timperley remarked upon in their 2007 paper on feedback.[21]

Pupil to teacher feedback

Instruction is more powerful when teachers welcome feedback from pupils about what they understand, where they are conscious of making mistakes and when they are engaged. Such openness makes clear to the pupils that feedback is important for everyone, teachers included. This is explored on pages 27–28.

Coaching as a form of feedback

Much of the literature on coaching talks about what might be called feed-forward as well as feedback. Feed-forward involves setting goals, planning strategies and visualising success as well as 'trying things out'. Two good books on the subject, *Encouraging children to learn* by Dinkmeyer and Dreikurs[22] and *Radical Encouragement* by Williams and Wegerif[23] offer similar advice:

■ Recognise and focus on pupils' strengths and assets.

■ Help pupils to define and achieve goals.

■ Be aware of the meanings pupils make of their experiences.

■ Recognise the differences between praise and encouragement.

It is also worth looking at the work of Paul Dearlove (www.stepupto.org) and Roger Greenaway (www.reviewing.co.uk), two of the UK's leading experts in techniques for coaching and reviewing.

Dialogue as a form of feedback

Dialogue is more than just speaking and listening – it is the very foundation for thinking. Lev Vygotsky, George Herbert Mead and, more recently, Matthew Lipman, have all argued in broad terms that:

■ Tasks we can jointly accomplish by talking together are gradually internalised so they become tasks we can achieve independently through our own thinking.

■ Thinking is rather like an internal dialogue. If we are exposed to rich, reflective dialogue, then characteristics of dialogue such as question and response manifest themselves in our own thinking, helping us to become more reflective. The implication is that if we regularly endure monologues from a teacher or parent with no invitation to question, then our own capacities for reflection will be limited.

Recognising the significance of this internal dialogue is an important step in improving the quality of feedback and, therefore, of learning. For if pupils do internalise aspects of dialogue with others, then it is important that our feedback provides a worthy model, capable of fostering positive, skilful and reflective thinking.

At the back of this book, there are many lesson ideas that aim to deepen and challenge learning through the use of dialogue. Using these ideas as a way of enhancing the quality of feedback in your classroom should have a very positive effect on pupil outcomes.

Further reading about dialogue

There are many strategies for feeding back through dialogue and for developing pupils' capacities for dialogue itself. Many well-established techniques such as 'talk partners' and 'think, pair, share' elicit peer feedback. However, the feedback teachers provide through dialogue is essential and the subject is broad and deep. I recommend the following books as starting points for a thorough, practical and theoretical understanding of the field:

- Alexander, R.J., *Towards Dialogic Teaching: Rethinking classroom talk*, Dialogos, 2004.
- Cam, P., *Thinking Together: Philosophical inquiry for the classroom*, Hale & Iremonger, 1995.
- Kagan, S., *Classbuilding: Cooperative learning activities*, Kagan Cooperative Learning, 1995.
- Wegerif, R., 'Dialogic education: what is it and why do we need it?', *Education Review*, 2006, Vol. 19, No.2.

Dialogue in a community of inquiry

One of the best ways to both provide feedback (through dialogue) and develop capacities for dialogue with your pupils is through working to develop a 'community of inquiry'.[24]

The 'community' aims for cooperation, care, respect and safety; the 'inquiry' reaches for understanding, meaning, truth and values supported by reasons.

If a community of inquiry develops successfully over time, pupils' questions get deeper and more thoughtful; their discussions are disciplined and focused yet, at the same time, imaginative. They care about what others say but don't accept easy answers; they give feedback on what they hear in the form of questions and challenges.

JNP

Philosophy for Children (P4C)

Doing Philosophy for Children (P4C) is the most direct way of bringing about a community of inquiry in the classroom. Begun in 1972 by Professor Matthew Lipman and colleagues at the IAPC (Institute for the Advancement of Philosophy for Children),[25] P4C is now a worldwide educational initiative, practised in more than sixty countries. Many of the practices of P4C transfer very well across the curriculum and contribute to developing feedback cultures in that they enable the following conditions of feedback to flourish:

Understanding the objective

At the beginning of a P4C session, a question is identified (there are many examples of the sorts of questions one might expect in the lesson plans, beginning on page 127). The inquiry then focuses the attention of the community on understanding the meaning(s) of the question and testing out answers. Objectives related to standards of reasoning and behaviour are applied, reviewed and amended on a regular basis.

Thinking through current understanding

Having begun an exploration of the question, participants in a community of inquiry are then encouraged to reflect on their own thinking, including beliefs and assumptions, and how these relate to other people's ideas.

Identifying ways to bridge the gap

During, and very often after, the initial inquiry, participants collaborate together to identify possible steps towards finding the best answer to a difficult question. In this way, P4C addresses the three crucial questions about feedback:

- What are we trying to achieve?
- Where are we now?
- What should our next steps be?

In addition, P4C introduces pupils to the following realities: there is not always an answer for every question and there is no shame in sometimes not realising one's goals.

An overview of P4C[26]

Practice 1: Encourage questioning

1 Encourage pupils to ask questions by incorporating a question–creation session in some of your lessons. Allow pupils to talk to a partner before coming up with their question. Get pupils to write their questions down.

2   Collect questions and study them with the pupils. Discuss the kinds of questions they are and how they could be answered. Display the questions and write them up in 'question book collections' or display them on the walls.

3   Make space and time in your lessons to discuss pupils' questions with them. Help pupils to spot assumptions and significant concepts contained in the questions.

4   Help pupils discriminate between those questions, or parts of questions, that require information, inference and considered judgement. So, for example, a story such as Little Red Riding Hood might prompt pupils to ask: 'What did the father warn the girl about?' (information). 'What happened to Grandma?' (inference). 'Should children always do what they are told?' (judgement).

5   Help pupils to choose questions they will discuss together (see Practice 3).

Practice 2: Develop concepts

Pick out some significant concepts (see pages 128–134) and make time to discuss them with pupils. Stimulate discussion by introducing some 'borderline cases', such as scenarios or questions involving the chosen concept in cases where it is not obviously suitable for application (e.g. Is deciding to give up smoking an instance of 'willpower'?). Allow pupils to explore their understanding and lead them to deeper levels in the discussion.

Practice 3: Encourage dialogue and argument

Here are some steps you can take to encourage dialogue and argument in your classes:

■   Have the pupils sit in a circle so they can see each other and listen in a more focused way.

■   Establish some ground rules for good dialogue and help pupils put them into practice.

■   Establish the idea of argument as a means towards finding the best answer to a question and through which possible answers are contested. Encourage pupils to argue without rancour by testing claims and reasons in a spirit of collaborative argument.

■   Give pupils thinking time by allowing short 'breakouts' where they can converse with a partner to gather their thoughts or rehearse their arguments.

■   Give pupils examples of the sorts of moves they can make to take the dialogue to a deeper level. These would include: thinking of alternative points of view and speculating about the consequences of different ones; giving examples; noticing similarities and differences; examining reasons; and establishing whether statements about people and things apply to all, many, some and/or none.

Practice 4: Work for reasonableness

If you have put in place all the features listed above, then your pupils should be well on the way to becoming reasonable in all senses of the word; they should be open to new ideas and alternative points of view, they shouldn't judge prematurely the opinions of others and they will tend to value arguments that are supported by reasons. If you value reasonableness and draw attention to its various aspects, then pupils are more likely to come to value it too. Information about P4C, resources and training are readily available on the web.[27]

> Carless (2006) asked students and teachers whether teachers provided detailed feedback that helped students improve their next assignments. About 70% of the teachers claimed they provided such detailed feedback often or always, but only 45% of students agreed with their teachers' claims.
>
> Further, Nuthall (2005) found that most feedback that students obtained in any day in classrooms was from other students, and most of this feedback was incorrect.
>
> (John Hattie, 2009)[28]

Formative and summative feedback

Formative assessment refers to ongoing, diagnostic assessment that helps pupils to make progress in their learning. Summative feedback, on the other hand, identifies only what the pupils have done right and what they have done wrong. It usually involves a grade or exit rating. Table 2.1 shows the main differences.

TABLE 2.1 Formative versus summative feedback

Confirmation	Your answer was right/wrong.	Summative assessment
Corrective	Your answer was incorrect. The right answer is . . .	
Explanatory	Your answer was incorrect because . . .	Formative assessment
Diagnostic	Your answer suggests you forgot to . . .	
	Next time, concentrate on the following before answering . . .	
Elaborative	Your answer was spot on.	
	A key to this was your decision to focus on . . .	
	To improve even more next time, I suggest you . . .	

Marking

What comes out loud and clear from the work of Robert Marzano *et al.*[29] and Professor Paul Black is that teacher-feedback should normally avoid giving marks.

> Research experiments have established that, whilst pupils' learning can be advanced by feedback through comments, the giving of marks, or grades, has a negative effect in that pupils ignore comments when marks are also given.
>
> And yet, like so many teachers, I was expected, when I was a teacher, to give marks or grades whenever I responded to a pupil's work. When I stopped this practice, many of my students questioned whether something was wrong. Some of their parents complained I wasn't marking properly – and even one or two heads of department advised me to return to standard practice as soon as possible.
>
> Over time though, my students did begin to read my comments and feedback more thoroughly. When I asked them why this was, they reported that previously, if they got 10 out of 10 or an A or B grade, then there was no point reading my comments because they knew they'd done well. Or, if they'd got a low grade or score, then they knew that they were useless, so what was the point in reading any further?
>
> (Black and Wiliam, 1998)[30]

If you are obliged to give grades, then perhaps alternate between giving marks for one set of assignments and giving useful comments on the next set. That way, the grades can be used for whatever purpose they are supposed to meet, and your comments can be used to support the learning process.

Example 'marking' by the author

Learning intention: To make better use of examples and counter-examples in your writing so that your conclusion is more considered.

Teacher's comments: 'Well done, Craig, you have made significant progress towards reaching the learning intention. There are now far more wide-ranging and thought-provoking examples to support your conclusions than in your earlier work. I particularly like the example you used in line 7 that suggests common sense isn't always right. What I'd like to see more of in your next piece of work is the use of counter-examples, as these will help to create a less biased tone to your conclusion.'

Questions to think about: 'Can you think of a counter-example that you might have used in this piece? Also, what might be some of the benefits of using counter-arguments in your next persuasive text?'

Table 2.2 summarises research into the impact of comments, as opposed to grading, of feedback to 132 11-year-olds (from impact of the use of grades in marking pupils' work, Butler).[31] The gains refer to pupils' achievement in a given subject area.

TABLE 2.2 Formative versus summative feedback

GROUP	FEEDBACK	PRE-POST GAIN	ATTITUDES
A	Comments only	30% gain	Positive
B	Grades only	No gain	Top 25% – Positive Bottom 25% – Negative
B	Grades and comments	No gain	Top 25% – Positive Bottom 25% – Negative

Mark alongside the pupil

The best way to mark work is together with the pupil who did the work. He or she can then offer insights into the decisions they made and you can coach them to identify ways to improve similar work next time. Timetabling a meeting with each pupil every fortnight, before or after school, helped me to be a more effective marker and teacher in several ways. First, it reduced dramatically the amount of time I spent marking at home. Second, it improved the effectiveness of my feedback – my presence guaranteed that comments were heard and the pupils were able to question me about my advice.

At Douglas Park School in Masterton, New Zealand, teachers have developed the use of a learning conference to enhance marking alongside pupils. I have written at length about this on my blog (www.challenginglearningblog.com) but, in short, their rationale is:

> 'Assess' comes from Latin, to sit beside, so our learning conferences give parents the perfect opportunity to 'sit beside' their child; to encourage our students to take personal responsibility for their learning; to develop their communication and organisational skills; to clarify for themselves and their parents their sense of progress and to further enhance the school-home communication and relationships.

Invite pupils to respond to your marking

If it is too difficult to find time for one-to-one feedback with each pupil, then shape your written comments in such a way as to invite a verbal or written response from them. See 'Example marking by the author' on page 20 for an example of this type of invitational comment.

Peer and self-reviews

If most of the feedback pupils receive comes from their peers and is incorrect,[32] then it would be imperative for pupils to be taught how to give, receive and act on quality feedback.

Simply having pupils review and analyse their own work and the work of others is not enough. They need guidance as to the nature and outcomes of appropriate review and analysis. Here are some examples I've collected from schools I've worked with over the last few years:

a) Self-assessment in maths

This example is from a Year 9 (14-year-olds) class taught by Lachlan Champion at Brighton Secondary College in Melbourne.

There are many aspects of this self-assessment sheet I like: first, the success criteria in the left-hand column leaves pupils in no doubt as to what they should be aiming to achieve.

Second, moving the 'faces' from the left-hand columns to the furthest right-hand column will give a real sense of progress. A snapshot (as per the example) will also show, at a glance, how a pupil is getting on and what his or her next steps should be.

If you take a look at the definition I gave on page 6, you will see how this self-assessment grid helps pupils to think about all three stages of feedback:

1   Understand the goal or learning intention.

2   Know where they are in relation to the goal.

Skill	Not shown	Sometimes shown	Mostly shown	Always shown
Recall the formula				☺
Label the triangle's sides				☺
Find the hypotenuse				☺
Rearrange the fumula to find a shorter side				☺
Solve compound shapes using diagrams		☐		
Answer worded questions (in a sentence)	☹			
Rounding off			☺	
Quality working out			☺	
Extension questions		☐		

FIGURE 2.2

3   Realise what they need to do to bridge the gap between the current position and the goal.

b) Self-assessment in history

This example is from a Year 11 (16-year-olds) class taught by Frank Egan at Aranmore Catholic College in Perth.

I had the great pleasure of working with the staff of Aranmore Catholic College in Perth in 2012. The same day we had worked together, one of the teachers – Frank Egan – designed the history self-assessment sheet seen in Figure 2.3.

Some of the comments Frank received as a result included:

- 'I can actually see how to improve, it's obvious.'
- 'I can see that I don't have enough facts in the paragraphs.'
- 'So a conclusion is that important?'
- 'My intro wasn't anywhere close to what is here.'

Also, as Frank wrote in an email to me soon after: 'One boy wanted to know why something so simple hadn't been shown before'.

	Not shown	Almost there	Completed	Completed and detailed
Introduction				
4+ sentences				
Proposition stated				
Outline of narrative				
Context of topic				
Body of essay				
3+ paragraphs				
6+ facts per paragraph				
Inter-relationships				
Argument is relevant				
Quote with source given				
Conclusion				
3+ sentences				
Summation				
Proof of proposition				
Literacy				
Spelling accuracy				
Grammar structures				
Use of synonyms				

FIGURE 2.3

c) Collecting past examples

Frank Egan's guide sheet above should help pupils improve their work to the point of being very good, but what about writing the very best essays? That presumably requires a certain *je ne sais quoi* not easily identified by mere bullet points.

To help with this, I encourage you to photocopy three examples of every piece of work you read – the very best example, a good example and an average example. You can then make the copies anonymous and encourage pupils in other year groups to analyse them.

For example, you could give the three examples (excellent, good, average), together with a guide sheet similar to Frank's, to a group and ask them to decide which essay is the best, which is good and which is just OK. Or you could mark the three examples and then ask pupils to create a self-assessment sheet based on the differences.

Of course this isn't restricted only to history essays; the same procedure could be used in any subject. For example, videoing three performances and identifying the differences (the medium could be sport, drama, music, dance or any combination of these); comparing three pieces of art; three poems; three ways to complete a scientific experiment, and so on. The important thing is that pupils will have varying standards with which to compare and contrast.

The 7 steps to feedback heaven

Since writing the first edition of this book, I have developed 'The 7 steps to feedback heaven'. This brings together what I believe to be the best aspects of feedback theory and practice.

The 7 steps to feedback heaven

1   Identify goals
2   First draft
3   Self and/or peer review
4   Second draft
5   Teacher feedback
6   Final draft
7   Grade (if needed)

1 Identify the goals

If your pupils don't understand their learning goals then feedback is not going to work very well. So do all you can to get this part right! I would go as far as to say that if your pupils don't understand their learning goals then do not bother with feedback about the task. Use encouragement, praise and refocusing techniques but don't bother with feedback; it is unlikely to be effective.

The history and maths examples on the previous pages are good examples of learning goals. With younger children, clarifying the goals might be something along the lines of:

> As we paint our pictures, there are two things I'd like you to concentrate on: 1) use the whole page (last week, a lot of you painted your pictures right down in the corner, leaving a lot of unused space), and 2) I'd like you to use at least three colours.

Remember: goal setting doesn't need to be reserved for 'curriculum' topics. For example, it could be done with swimming.

> As you practise your freestyle, there are two key things I want you to concentrate on: make sure your elbow is the first part of your arm to exit the water (not your hand or shoulder); and do not over-rotate your head when turning to breathe – just turn your head enough to allow half of your mouth to breathe.

Or, with group work:

> While working in groups, I'd like you to pause intermittently to give each other feedback about: giving reasons; connecting to what other people have said; and showing that you are listening as others are talking.

2 First draft (or first go if doing a physical activity)

Once your pupils understand their learning goals – and what they should be able to do to show that learning – then they can make a start on their work. Encourage them to say they are doing their 'first draft' rather than their work. 'First draft' implies that there will be some editing to follow, whereas 'doing their work' could lead a pupil to think they've finished the whole process as soon as their first attempt is complete. The same is true when engaging in physical learning: encourage pupils to say they are making their first attempt rather than they are doing their performance. Again, this will lead to the assumption that there will be feedback and improvements to follow.

3 Self and/or peer assessment

After draft 1 is complete, pupils should then take time to review their work. This can be done individually or together with a response partner or classmate. Self-assessment involves pupils comparing their first draft against the learning intentions and success criteria, so that they can answer the key feedback questions:

1   What am I trying to achieve?
2   How much progress have I made so far?
3   What should I do next?

4 Second draft (or second go if doing a physical activity)

Following on from the advice they receive from their response partner – or based on their own reflections when comparing their first draft against their success criteria – pupils should then improve and re-draft their work. I do not mean that they should do it all again. I mean they should make additions and corrections – perhaps in a different colour if they are doing a written task, by engaging 'markup' if doing something electronically, or by trying the skill once more if they are engaged in some 'physical' learning.

5 Teacher feedback

Once your pupils have completed steps 1 to 4 then it is time for some teacher-led feedback. Of course, we might have been giving feedback, guidance and encouragement throughout the process, but stage 5 of the feedback steps is when we should give our more formalised feedback.

There are many conventions popular in schools but I would say the most effective guidelines are that feedback should include advice, advice, advice. In other words: what could be changed, amended, left alone, added to, scrapped altogether?

The advice should be very obviously focused on the task rather than on the student (e.g., 'clarify the conclusion by shortening your sentences and making them more punchy' rather than 'there is some need for clarity here. I want you to try harder'). For more about this, see the section on Carol Dweck's research later in the book.

Remember: teacher comments should be made as if you are the coach, not as if you are the referee! For example, we should be challenging, suggesting, encouraging, praising and demanding – all at the same time. Our feedback should push/encourage pupils beyond what they have been able to do by themselves. In other words, our feedback should get them into their Zone of Proximal Development (ZPD or 'wobble zone'). That is the whole point of feedback – to take pupils beyond what they are able to do by themselves; to stretch them beyond their current ability so that they make more progress.

Some teachers have actually said to me: 'Isn't it cheating to show kids how to improve their work?' My response is always: 'I'm sorry, I think you're confusing "cheating" with "teaching"!' Our *raison d'être* for working with pupils is to help them go beyond what they can do by themselves! Feedback should help pupils to improve and do better than they can by themselves. Of course we are not allowed to do this with assessed pieces of coursework. But with all other pieces of work, feedback is one of the best tools in our toolbox for helping students to make outstanding progress.

Please note – do NOT give a grade or mark yet; if grades are needed then these should be held back until step 7.

6 Final draft (or final performance if doing a physical activity)

Here's the key to the 7 steps to feedback heaven: your pupils should complete their final draft after your feedback, not before it!

How many times do we give feedback to pupils after they've finished their work? What is the point of that? I know we give advice ready for the next time they do a similar activity, but honestly though, how many pupils say: 'Great! I can't wait to have another go at this topic just so that I can use these wonderful words of wisdom from my teacher?' Maybe your pupils do say that! If so then you teach very different pupils to the ones I've ever taught. As far as I know, my pupils have only ever nodded, at best, or dismissed, at worst, the comments that I've made after they'd finished their work.

The whole point of feedback is that it should modify the performance or learning of the pupil. So let's get the timing right and give our wonderful, thought-provoking and insightful feedback before pupils finish their work (though not before they've gone through stages 2, 3 and 4 first).

7 Grade (if needed)

It is a well-rehearsed argument that grades do very little for the learning process. Indeed, as Ruth Butler (see Table 2.2) and others have pointed out, grades often diminish the power of feedback to the point that giving feedback together with grades is the equivalent of giving no feedback at all!

However, if you are required to grade work, then make it work for you: get your pupils to grade their own work. If they are very accurate with this, then job done. If they are not, then you will receive some very useful information about what they do and don't understand about the success criteria. Indeed, I have found that when I tell pupils at the beginning of a task that they will be expected to grade their own work, they tend to take much more notice of the success criteria! So perhaps grading can be put to good effect after all?

Whether or not you get your pupils to grade their own (or each other's) work, the key is that the grading should be kept separate from the formative feedback you are giving at stage 5 of the process.

Some notes about the 7 steps to feedback heaven

When I started out as a teacher, it was commonplace for leaders to visit classrooms to watch teachers teach. This always seemed to be the wrong emphasis: why focus on the teaching when surely it's the learning that matters most? Far too often, teaching doesn't lead to the intended learning – and sometimes even gets in the way of learning. Whereas at other times, the best learning takes place when there is no teaching!

Thankfully things have moved on since then and now it is far more commonplace for leaders to observe *learning* (often asking pupils the three key feedback questions: what are you learning; how much progress have you made; and what are your next steps?)

However, things don't seem to have moved on so quickly when it comes to feedback: we are still looking at the feedback itself rather than the effect of the feedback. By this I mean that feedback is the transmission of a message (in the same way that teaching is the transmission of a message,) whereas the impact of feedback is how that message is understood and applied (in the same way that learning is how a message is understood and applied).

So, we should not be looking at the quality of feedback – particularly as this so often becomes an obsession with the quality of 'marking'. Instead, we should be looking at the impact of the feedback. Why so many schools insist on having 'marking policies' showing how to mark and when to mark is beyond me. Wouldn't it be better to create 'Learning from Feedback' policies that seek to examine the impact of teacher feedback?

To do this, we could use a coding system that makes it easy to identify what constitutes draft 1, what constitutes draft 2 and then what are the final edits. Something as straightforward as colour coding in which draft 1 is in black, edits that make up draft 2 are in red and final edits are in green would work. Or using the mark-up tool in e-docs would do just as well.

The main point is that we ought to be able to see the impact of a pupil's self-assessment by looking at the edits they made to move from draft 1 to draft 2, and then the impact of our feedback by looking at the edits they made between draft 2 and their final draft. In so doing, we'd be looking at what really matters: the impact of feedback, not the feedback itself.

This would then free us from the tyranny of having to write feedback as much for the benefit of the person checking our work as for the benefit of the student whose book we're 'marking'. It would also move us back to what we all know – that some of the best feedback pupils receive is verbal – or even non-verbal (such as a gesture of encouragement or redirection). Written feedback can be very useful of course – particularly if given before a student finishes their piece of work. But to suggest, as so many 'marking policies' do, that written feedback is the only type that counts is simplistic at best, and absolutist at worst.

Teach pupils how to give feedback

Pupils should be taught how to give feedback. More often than not, their starting point will be to imitate the ways their teachers have given them feedback – hence the need to get our practice right. After that, a few guidelines such as the ones at the end of this chapter will help to improve the quality and effectiveness of peer-to-peer assessments.

I present three models in this book: the ASK model: attitudes, skills and knowledge (see pages 34–36), the Teaching Target model (TTM see pages 53–56) and the Learning Pit model (see pages 109–126). To make the best use of these models, I recommend that you:

Create opportunities for self-reflection

The average amount of time a teacher waits after asking a question is 1 second or less! This effectively closes off the possibility for pupils to reflect on the question or prepare their response. So, the first thing must be to slow down, leave time for thinking, and not be tempted to fill in silences with repeated questions or prompts to get pupils to talk prematurely. The 1-second figure comes from Mary Budd Rowe, who in 1973 observed benefits ensuing from the practice of increasing the wait time after asking a question from the average of less than 1 second to waiting 3 seconds:

- The length of explanations among advantaged groups increased fivefold and among disadvantaged groups sevenfold.
- The number of unsolicited but appropriate comments dramatically increased.
- Failures to respond decreased from an average of 30 per cent to less than 5 per cent.
- The number of questions asked by children rose sharply.

(Mary Budd Rowe at the Department of Childhood Education, University of Florida)[33]

I created the peer review template to help my pupils learn how to review each other's work and then their own. It is based on the ASK model I used for reviewing and previewing (pages 42–44), and on Carol Dweck's growth mindsets (explored on pages 45–47). The templates are intended to be used by pupils working in pairs. It is important to discuss the terminology used in the templates with pupils so they are not used in too judgemental a way but as a tool to explore learning. You may also need to adapt the language depending on the age of the pupils.

If pupils are to become competent assessors of their own work, as developments in metacognition tell us they should, then they need sustained experience in ways of questioning and improving the quality of their work, and supported experience in assessing their work in addition to understanding what counts as the standard expected and criteria on which they will be assessed.

(Royce Sadler, 1989)[34]

Peer review template (ASK)

A – Attitudes

Completely focused

My partner is completely absorbed in this new learning, is taking creative risks to extend their understanding and is trying to work out how the learning will apply to other contexts.

Determined

My partner is determined to learn, is focused on making progress and is beginning to think through the meaning of the new learning.

Interested

My partner is interested in the learning but is struggling and wants to achieve the skill and knowledge necessary to understand it.

Uninterested but willing

My partner is not really interested in the learning but is having a go at it.

Uninterested and unwilling

My partner shows no signs of interest in the topic as yet and is not willing to have a go.

S – Skills

Highly skilled

My partner displays outstanding skill, makes no significant errors and can perform the skill almost automatically.

Proficient

My partner can perform the skill or process in a very capable manner.

Practised

My partner is well-practised and able to perform the skill quite well now.

Developing

There are some signs that my partner is beginning to learn and develop the skill.

Beginner

My partner hasn't moved beyond the beginner/novice stage yet.

K – Knowledge

A thorough understanding

My partner knows about and fully understands this new learning and is able to explain its wider significance to others.

A good understanding

My partner can give some good answers about the learning in response to questions beginning with what, why, when and how.

A basic understanding

My partner can give a basic answer to each what, why, when and how question but with little detail.

One or two ideas

My partner has a bit of knowledge about the topic but cannot explain things yet.

No knowledge

My partner doesn't seem to have any knowledge about this topic yet.

Praise

Although it is often the most pleasant form of feedback to give and receive, praise has its pitfalls. Carol Dweck, whose research has been quoted throughout this book, suggests that praising pupils for their intelligence can make it more likely they will fear failure and cope poorly with setbacks.[35]

Professor Dweck's work identifies and examines two types of personal goals: performance goals (such as achieving good grades or being recognised as successful) and learning goals (intentions to learn). Dweck refers to these as fixed mindset and growth mindset, respectively. Praise often feeds the fixed mindset to the detriment

of learning. I explore Dweck's work on mindsets further in the chapter on Application (pages 45–47).

Furthermore, research by Greene and Miller (1996) found that a focus on performance goals tended to lead to shallow processing and therefore low achievement, whereas possession of learning-related goals in combination with high self-esteem led to meaningful cognitive engagement and higher achievement.[36]

Praise is covered in depth in the Self-esteem chapter, beginning on page 97. However, here is an overview of my main recommendations:

- Praise actions rather than the individual (e.g. 'lovely reading' rather than 'lovely reader').
- Ensure praise is specific and relates to progress rather than innate ability.
- Avoid comparing one pupil with another.
- Keep praise credible (avoid insincere or 'pity praise').
- Praise meaningful success, rather than pupils' success on tasks that are easy for them.

Pupil-to-teacher feedback

> When teachers seek, or at least are open to, feedback from students as to what students know, what they understand, where they make errors, when they have misconceptions, when they are not engaged – then teaching and learning can be synchronised and powerful.
>
> (John Hattie, 2009)[37]

In addition to the multi-directional feedback that comes with the sort of reflective dialogue I described earlier, rich feedback from pupils can be instigated by the following questions from the teacher:

- What helps you to learn the most?
- What helps you to concentrate in class?
- What do you really want to make progress with in this year?
- How do you know when you have made progress?
- What type of group work helps you to learn the most?
- What could I do to help you learn more?
- What could you do to help yourself learn more?

Teachers learn from these responses to make their own ongoing targets. It is important to note, however, that often the first answer from a pupil can be superficial, so it is important to keep probing with subsequent questions until rich data is generated from which to plan further teaching interventions.

An excellent example of this was when my 10-year-old pupils told me, after a prolonged period of questioning, that they learnt most when I asked difficult, open questions. This prompted me to create an open-questions list to have by my side during lessons (see pages 129–134 for a similar list). After just a few uses of this list, my pupils asked if they could have a copy which they then used to improve their own questioning techniques. This was one of the key factors in the excellent progress they made that year.

Video and computer feedback

Though I have no data other than anecdotal evidence to support this claim, it appears that pupils trust, and respond positively to feedback given by a computer. Negative feedback from a computer about a particular task – 'No, that is the wrong solution!' – is taken to apply only to the current performance, rather than as a slight on the pupil as a person or learner. In contrast, many pupils take negative feedback from an adult as personal criticism.

Reviewing performance and behaviour using video evidence is a particularly vivid and powerful form of feedback. Used frequently in teacher mentoring, but increasingly as a way to review the day's learning with young children, video evidence allows learners to reflect on the quality of such things as their listening, the quality of their attention and their support for others, and to talk openly about ways to improve in the future.

Top 10 FACTS for feedback

1 Begin with the understanding of clear and specific goals

Identify goals at the beginning of a task by agreeing learning intentions, success criteria and/or previewing benchmark targets. Then refer to these and not to other superficial features of pupils' performance. Comments such as 'good' or 'well done' are of little use unless they are supported by target-specific information.

2 Encourage pupils to consider where they are in relation to a learning goal

For a goal to be a 'learning goal', it needs to be beyond what the pupil can do or understand at the time. Pupils should be able to acknowledge that failing to achieve a goal at the first time of trying is a common, and even essential, part of their learning.

3 Avoid comparisons that do not foster growth

Comparing the achievement of one pupil with another will not give either of them the information they need in order to grow. The best comparative information pupils can get is in relation to their own previous performance.

4 Ensure feedback is formative

A key factor that distinguishes feedback from praise is the intention to be formative. So, identify what pupils have achieved, what has been preventing them from achieving their learning goals and what they could do to improve further.

5 Keep feedback well-timed

Feedback is most effective when pupils are still able to reflect upon the decisions they made during a task they undertook. Once pupils forget what they did and why, feedback loses its potency.

6 Refer to progress rather than ability

Praising ability or intelligence can lead to a fear of failure and personal fragility (Carol Dweck)[38] so give feedback relative to progress only.

7 Do not avoid tests but get the timing right and use them formatively

According to research by Marzano *et al.*,[39] giving a test one day after a learning situation will be most useful, though Professor Paul Black[40] suggests that testing one week after the initial learning is best. Either way, the most effective way to use tests is to begin a subsequent, connected lesson by testing what the pupils have learned in previous lessons and use this data to create further learning objectives.

8 When marking the tests, do not give scores or grades

The giving of marks or grades has a negative effect on learning because pupils then ignore any supporting comments (Black and Wiliam).[41] So use comments related to progress and subsequent targets instead.

9 Think of yourself as a 'coach' rather than a 'referee'

As we know, a referee's main task is to uphold the rules of the game; whereas a coach should support, encourage, demonstrate, stretch, challenge and motivate players towards better performance. When giving feedback, think of yourself as that coach!

10 Teach pupils how to give, act on and receive quality feedback

Pupils can monitor effectively their own progress and that of a partner once they have been shown how. This is vital for learning, particularly considering that most feedback pupils receive is from their peers. Creating a learning environment in which pupils can develop self-regulation and error-detection skills will further enhance the significance of feedback on the learning process.

3

Application

FEEDBACK
APPLICATION
CHALLENGE
THINKING
SELF-ESTEEM

> 'Mediocrity achieves more with application than superiority does without it.'
> Baltasar Gracián y Morales, 1601–1658
> (author of *The Art of Worldly Wisdom*)

Application key points

Definition

Pupils apply themselves when they pay close attention to their learning and persist in their efforts. The extent to which they apply themselves to a learning goal often depends on the value they ascribe to the goal multiplied by the level of expectation they have of achieving it.

Importance

Application to learning is one of the key factors in determining how much progress a pupil will make. Consider the many 'mediocre' talents who, through application and belief, have excelled in life, including:

- Winston Churchill, who twice failed the Royal Military Academy's entrance exam before leading Britain to victory with her allies in World War Two;

- Walt Disney, who was fired by a newspaper editor because he 'lacked imagination';

■ Norma Jean Baker, who was told by the director of the Blue Book Modelling Agency that she had 'better learn secretarial work or else get married', before recreating herself as Marilyn Monroe.

Be wary of

Be wary of assuming that particular pupils either do or do not have the capacity to apply themselves. Application is more likely to be an outcome of motivation and belief rather than genetics.

Application

According to the work of Wigfield and Eccles on the Expectancy-Value theory (2000) (see Figure 3.1), pupils' application to a task will be determined by how much they value the learning goal, multiplied by how much they expect to achieve the goal.[43]

The term 'multiplied' is important here – if desire is zero, then the likely application will be zero, no matter how high the expectancy 'score' is. Similarly, application is likely to be zero if expectancy is zero, even if desire is great.

FIGURE 3.1 Application = value x expectancy

From Wigfield and Eccles, 'Expectancy-Value theory of achievement motivation'.[42]

Valuing learning goals

How much do your pupils value the learning goals that are set for them, and how often do you 'broadcast' in the W I I – FM channel? (What's In It For Me?)

Aside from the power of persuasion and the use of real-life, contemporary issues to bring the curriculum alive, I have found the following four methods – discussed in more detail in this chapter – to be effective in increasing the extent to which the pupils value learning:

- considering the curriculum as a context for learning how to learn;
- developing holistic education with the help of the ASK model;
- using the (P)Review strategy to increase the sense of ownership and meaning;
- developing 'growth' mindsets.

> We now accept the fact that learning is a lifelong process of keeping abreast of change. And the most pressing task is to teach people how to learn.
> (Peter Drucker, 1909–2005, described by *Business Week* as 'the man who invented management')[44]

Learning how to learn

'I believe I'm here to help you become the best learners you can be.'

That's what I have explained to every group of pupils I've ever taught. It is a belief that is central to my book. I also think it helps raise the value of learning in pupils' minds. For if I can persuade them that a key purpose of education is to learn how to learn, then it follows that they should sometimes expect to learn things they don't want to learn.

I realise, of course, that education isn't only about learning how to learn. Acquiring knowledge, skills and attitudes should be a harmonious activity with each component playing its part. In order to learn how to learn, one must learn something; and it is better that the something be valuable rather than trivial or even harmful. The problem is that if we focus too much on knowledge and over-help children to acquire it (in order to pass the tests) and focus too little on skills and attitudes, then we disable pupils from learning how to learn, rather than enabling them.

By an effort of refocusing, we can still teach the knowledge that we value but also enable pupils to learn by, for example, asking relevant questions, persisting with challenges, withstanding temporary setbacks, being systematic in their thinking, speculating about alternatives (e.g. ways of solving a problem or interpretations of history) and tracking consequences (i.e. of applying different alternatives). We should also explore with them, as part of the programme of extending their knowledge, the concepts that underlie all subjects, such as evidence, cause, truth, beauty, experiment, interpretation, fact and so on.

The ASK model

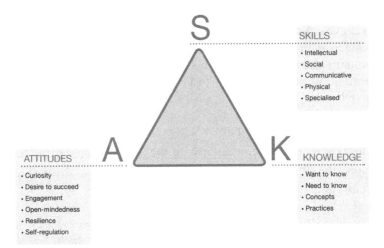

FIGURE 3.2 The ASK model

If we can teach the curriculum more slowly and with greater attention to attitudes, skills and concepts, then we can speed up the rate at which the pupils can learn the curriculum because the preconditions for learning new topics will already be in place. They can do much of the factual learning themselves.

So what does learning how to learn mean?

Outstanding learners have positive attitudes, are skilful in a number of aspects of learning, have good general knowledge and conceptual understanding and are able to find and assess information. Therefore, to grow into an expert learner, pupils need to develop in at least three domains:

- **Attitudes** – positive attitudes towards learning, including curiosity and persistence
- **Skills** – abilities to carry out those processes necessary for gaining understanding, taking part in dialogue and achieving excellent performance in any given field
- **Knowledge** – familiarity with information, concepts, theories and practices in a given field.

To help my pupils grow in each of these domains, I developed the ASK model, a graphic illustration in the form of a triangle (see Figure 3.2). I have also used it myself as a tool for planning, review and, latterly, feedback. Each of these functions are explored in Figures 3.2 and 3.4, and in the peer review template on pages 24–26.

An overview of the ASK model

To become successful learners then, pupils need to develop attitudes such as mindfulness, diligence and curiosity; to develop skills such as reasoning, inquiry and collaborative thinking skills; and to be able to draw on and apply an increasing store of knowledge. To see how I have broken down each domain, take a look at pages 36–40 for attitudes, page 41 for skills, and pages 41–42 for knowledge.

Drawing out attitudes relating to self

Sample answers:

Examples from 7-year-olds

Trying my best

Being willing to be helped

Concentrating hard

Having a go

Not giving up

Not fretting about mistakes

Asking questions

Examples from 11-year-olds

Always trying hard

Being open to advice

Thinking carefully

Being willing to try new things

Never-say-die attitude

Learning from mistakes

Being curious

Examples from 14-year-olds

Persevering

Being open to support and coaching

Being focused on what's relevant

Being open to new experiences

Resilience

Treating mistakes as useful feedback

Enquiring and being curious

At the core of every true talent there is an awareness of the difficulties inherent in any achievement, and the confidence that by persistence and patience something worthwhile will be realised. Thus talent is a species of vigour.

(Eric Hoffer, 1902–1983, American dockworker and philosopher)

Think of the difference between teaching thirty pupils who value learning and fifteen pupils who don't. Or compare the likely progress of a child who is easily discouraged, with one who persists and overcomes challenges. It seems attitudes play a major role in the outcomes of education.

Many believe that a combination of genetic disposition and upbringing will determine the extent to which pupils value learning. They argue that we can only work with or against what is already given. Instead, I believe that we can modify the given by modelling, articulating and encouraging attitudes we know will motivate pupils to learn.

That is easier said than done, of course, since finding agreement about which attitudes are the 'right' ones to promote is a challenge in itself. For sources of inspiration, I highly recommend Art Costa's *Habits of Mind*,[45] and Guy Claxton's *Building Learning Power*.[46]

My favoured approach, however, is to draw out ideas from pupils. To do this, I would ask them to consider the following:

- Think of a goal or target that you have achieved; for example, learning to ride your bike, reciting your times tables, playing a musical instrument, writing a poem, making friends at a new school
- What attitudes helped you to achieve this?

Sample answers from different-aged pupils are shown above. There is also a selection of quotes on page 49 that might help your pupils to generate more ideas about positive attitudes to learning and to life.

Record the answers that the pupils come up with and turn these into statements of intent (see below for further exploration of this idea).

Class attitudes, not rules

Once attitudes relating to personal learning have been drawn out, it is worth asking pupils to add attitudes relating to social interaction – for example, respecting the right to opinions or silence, being open-minded and inclusive and so on. The full set can then be turned into a set of class attitudes.

For example, using the ideas offered by the 11-year-olds:

Sample answers from 11-year-olds

Always trying hard

Being open to advice

Thinking carefully

Being willing to try new things

Never-say-die attitude

Learning from mistakes

Staying focused

Open-minded

Corresponding statements of intent

We always try hard

We are open to advice, offering support to each other

We think carefully about our studies

We are willing to try new things

We are tenacious (have a 'never-say-die' attitude)

We treat mistakes as opportunities to learn

We concentrate and remain focused during our learning

We are open to new ideas and different opinions

And whatever you do, don't touch that computer!'

It is worth noting that engaging in dialogue about a set of class attitudes, regularly amending them and reviewing their application, diminishes the need for class rules which in itself is a good thing because:

- Rules are often counterproductive. For example, if a teacher warned her class: 'please don't mess around while I'm out and, whatever you do, don't touch that computer', what is the first thing that pupils would want to do?

- Psychological research and common sense suggest that motivation to reach a desired outcome often has more force than willingness to abide by prohibitive rules.

Articulate, model and encourage attitudes

It is not enough simply to decide the attitudes you wish to develop and then display them in the classroom. If that was all it took, then every school with pretty dispositions posters (e.g., TEAM: Together Everyone Achieves More, and the like) would have perfect pupils with perfect attitudes.

So, to have a better chance of embedding the attitudes you want, I suggest the following actions:

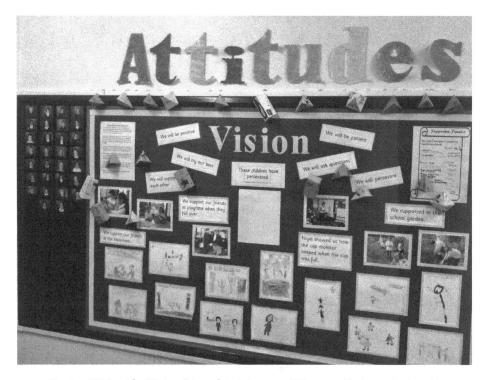

Teaching attitudes at Sandringham Primary School, Doncaster, UK (www.sandringham.vschool.org.uk)

1   Identify the attitudes that you wish to focus on, using the approach on pages 36–37.

2   Display these attitudes on the wall and talk with your pupils about their meanings. This would include developing from straightforward definitions to elaborations including:

- pupils creating a poster to illustrate each of the attitudes;
- identifying key role models for each attitude (e.g., Winston Churchill or Ellen MacArthur for tenacity);
- exploring each attitude through storytelling, poetry, art or philosophical inquiry.

3   Model each of the attitudes explicitly so it is obvious to your pupils how and when you are using each one to accomplish your (learning) goals.

4   Use every opportunity that presents itself to remind your pupils of the learning attitudes. For example, when they are stuck on a piece of work, remind them that this is an opportunity to practise perseverance.

5   Teach each of the attitudes as part of your learning intentions, using the ASK model.

Most skills that pupils need for learning are identified in the national curriculum of their country. However, above, I have outlined what I believe are the skills pupils need to become proficient learners. The categorisation provides you with a vision of 'an able learner' to share and discuss with colleagues.

SKILLS

Skills are the abilities to carry out those processes necessary for gaining understanding, taking part in dialogue and achieving excellent performance in any given field. Children (and adults) develop their abilities through social interaction and from the social, cultural and educational context of their lives.

GENERAL SKILLS			SPECIFIC SKILLS	
Intellectual	**Social**	**Communicative**	**Physical**	**Specialised**
Including ability to identify, model and alter relationships or concepts; understanding relevance; drawing conclusions; comparing and contrasting; asking relevant questions; and hypothesising	Including building rapport; respecting others' viewpoints; acting appropriately in particular contexts; self-regulation; working individually & as a team; and encouraging others	Including ability to understand and be understood; listening and responding appropriately to others; talking persuasively requesting things politely; paying full attention to a speaker; reading body language	Including Co-ordinated actions needed for such things as: penmanship; manipulating objects to represent ideas; catching and throwing an object; dancing; drama; riding a bicycle; making art; and playing a sport	Including Abilities we need for specific types of action such as using: a map and compass; a ruler or tape measure; a paint brush; sporting equipment; some weighing scales; a computer mouse; and driving a car

FIGURE 3.3 Classification of skills

'Can Amal come out to develop his attitudes, skills and knowledge?'

Intellectual abilities are explored in much greater depth in the Thinking chapter, beginning on page 77.

I've included social skills because although many people will say that getting on with others is more to do with attitude than skill, I'm not sure this is the case. I think both attitudes and skills affect behaviour. For example, a child may have a very friendly disposition but not, as yet, the ability to make friends. And of course the reverse might also be true; a child may know perfectly well how to make friends but not have the inclination to do so.

Thus, a lesson focusing on how to build rapport with another person, or how to begin a conversation with another person, will develop very important life skills that many pupils have yet to learn.

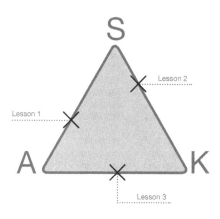

FIGURE 3.4 Teaching with the ASK model

Teaching with the ASK model

Each lesson is planned to incorporate two of the three domains, ensuring that over the course of the week, or term, there is a balance of objectives relating to ASK – thereby ensuring that the goal of holistic learning is pursued in a systematic way.

For example, referring to Figure 3.4, where lesson intention (LI) is given in the examples below, a series of lessons might be:

Lesson 1:

A balance between an attitude and a skill

LI: To exercise our curiosity (attitude: curiosity) by coming up with at least nine relevant questions (skill: asking relevant questions) about Vikings' lifestyles.

Lesson 2 (or part 2):

A skill takes priority, with knowledge as a secondary aim

LI: To decide which of the questions about Vikings has the most relevance to our topic (skill: prioritising by value) and will help us to know most about lifestyles (knowledge: the lifestyles of Vikings).

Lesson 3:

A balance between knowledge and an attitude

LI: To persist (attitude: persistence) in trying to find answers (knowledge: the particular answers) to the three fundamental questions about Vikings that we identified last time.

Note that the 'curriculum' is being taught throughout each lesson. Also, note that the cross to mark Lesson 2 on the diagram is purposely off-centre to denote a priority being placed on, in this case, skill. Thus, by the end of the week or term, there should be a good spread of crosses right around the triangle.

Knowledge

Presumably every curriculum in the world identifies the subject knowledge to be taught to pupils. However, a useful way to increase the pupils' sense of involvement in the curriculum and therefore their motivation to apply themselves to learning is to use 'preview' sessions.

When I taught primary children, we would use most of Friday afternoon for what we called the (P)Review Session (because it involved review and preview).

In secondary school, we would spend 5–10 minutes at the end of each lesson and then a full lesson at the end of each unit of work to preview the work that would follow. Of all the strategies I used as a teacher, the (P)Review was certainly one of the most significant.

Review and preview

Review

The first part involves reviewing, using the ASK framework, what has already been learned. For example:

- **Attitudes:** Pupils identified the values that had helped them reach their goals that week, giving reasons.
- **Skills:** Pupils demonstrated, to the whole class or to each other, the skills they had been working on that week.
- **Knowledge:** In groups, the pupils wrote five questions based on information we had covered during the week or unit of work. Each set of five questions was then used for our weekly quiz. Extra points were awarded to groups asking difficult questions that no other group could answer.

Preview

Having reviewed our learning, we'd then move on to previewing the following week or unit by considering the ASK we would focus on.

- **Attitudes and Skills:** We would first talk about these in light of the progress we'd been making. Then pupils would set themselves targets for the following week: for example, aiming to ask relevant questions or to consider a number of options before making decisions.
- **Knowledge:** We would preview the following week by considering for each forthcoming topic:
  - What would we *like* to know about the topic?
  - What do we *need* to know about the topic, so that we have a thorough understanding of it?

  So, for example, I would say that we were going to begin a new topic on tourism the following week, then ask, a) what the pupils *wanted* to know about tourism, and b) what they thought we *should* know about tourism by the end of the unit. We then listed the questions on the board, grouped them into units of work (or lesson plans) and, if there was time, began to do some initial research.

There are a great many benefits to previewing, including:

1 **Pupils planning with their teacher.** When pupils learn how to plan, assess and decide what's important, they also find ownership and motivation for their learning.

2 **Pupils prepare themselves for lessons.** Every time I previewed a lesson or topic, I asked my pupils to do some preparatory research. This helped them to be ready to begin the next lesson with their own further questions and comments. To start with, only the already-keen pupils would take this opportunity. Over time, though, all pupils realised the potential for progress that previewing offered and so joined in.

3 **Parents are more involved**. I've lost count of the number of parents and grandparents who've thanked me for previewing because this helped them to know how to help their own children, particularly when their children would rush home wanting help with research or wanting to know what Granddad knows about spiders' habitats (see pages 43–44 for the relevance of spiders' habitats).

4 **Teachers are more able to challenge and differentiate accurately.** By realising what the pupils already know and what they are wondering about, teachers have more data from which to plan and prepare future lessons.

5 **There is more time for challenge.** Over the course of a year, pupils spend no more than 20 per cent of their waking hours in lessons, as the calculation below shows! So time spent preparing for forthcoming lessons, while not in school, adds to the total learning time. It also permits more lesson time to be spent on getting pupils into the Learning Pit (see Chapter 7).

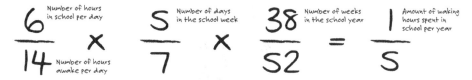

Calculation showing the proportion of waking hours in a school in a year

Spiders and their habitats

One story I often tell about previewing came from a group of 8–9 year olds previewing a new topic of 'habitats'. What followed went something along the lines of:

ME:	Does anyone know what a habitat is?
STEPHEN:	It's a furniture shop.
ME:	Yes, very good, but why do you suppose a furniture shop would be called 'habitat'?

We then had a discussion about furnishings, homes, and where we live.

ME: So, now we have some idea of what a habitat is, let's think of a creature that we can study in its habitat.

After going through all manner of options, including rats and snakes, we settled on 'spiders'.

ME: What do we want to know about spiders and their habitats?

CHILDREN: How many homes do they have? Are their webs their homes? Do they move nests a lot? How many spiders live in one habitat? Why are people scared of spiders?

ME: OK, great. Now, what questions do we need to answer to find out as much as we can about spiders and their habitats?

After a quick look at the topic books and a peek at the scheme of work, they came up with questions about climate, environment, food sources and predators. The children continued to preview at home before returning the next day with lots of information and stories about spiders. One boy even came back with a great joke about spiders, though sadly it's too rude to print here. You'll just have to listen to one of my keynotes to hear the punchline.

JMP.

Achievement is more likely to be increased when students invoke learning rather than performance strategies, accept rather than discount feedback, benchmark to difficult rather than to easy goals, compare themselves to subject criteria rather than to other students, possess high rather than low efficacy to learning, and effect self-regulation and personal control rather than learned helplessness in the academic situation. The willingness to invest in learning, to gain a reputation as a learner, and to show openness to experiences are the key dispositional factors that relate to achievement.

(John Hattie, 2009)[47]

Carol Dweck's theory of fixed and growth mindset

A significant factor influencing how well pupils apply themselves is their belief about intelligence. Carol Dweck's research has revealed that we all hold beliefs about concepts such as intelligence, ability and personality, with roughly half of us holding a 'fixed' theory and the other half a 'growth' theory of intelligence; Dweck calls these theories 'mindsets' and claims that people's application and success in learning is significantly affected by the particular mindset they adopt.

Those of us with a **fixed mindset** believe that innate, natural ability or talent determines our level of success. We enjoy success, even if we have succeeded with very little effort, and avoid setbacks and challenges.

Those of us with a **growth mindset** believe that factors such as effort, application and study skills will more accurately determine our level of success. We also enjoy success, but only really if we've had to work for what we perceive to be meaningful success.

This difference in mindset leads to varying levels of application: pupils with a fixed mindset will readily apply themselves when they perceive the chance of success to be high, avoiding any significant challenges; whereas pupils with a growth mindset will also relish situations in which the chance of learning, of encountering new and interesting challenges, is high.

This theory of mindset is explored in greater depth in the following pages, but for further information I recommend Carol Dweck's books: *Self theories*[48] and *Mindset*.[49]

Fixed mindset

Beliefs

- Intelligence and ability are fixed.
- Nature determines intelligence and ability.
- I have an innate ability for some things and an innate disability for other things.
- I will always be good at, for example, maths and always be poor at, for example, art.

Priority

- Prove myself.
- Succeed, especially with little effort, as this proves I am clever and/or able.
- Avoid failure of any sort, as this proves I have low ability levels.

Attitude to challenging learning

- Challenge should be avoided.
- Difficulties will mean I'm not as clever as I thought.
- Failure means I'm stupid or incapable.

I apply myself when there is . . .

- An opportunity to show off my strengths.
- A good chance of getting everything right.
- Very little risk of failure.

Response to challenge

- Blame myself or, to protect my ego, blame someone else.
- Feel inferior or incapable.
- Try guessing the answers or copying others.
- Seek ego-boosting distractions.

Mottos

- Either you're good at something or you're not.
- If you're really good at something, you shouldn't need to try.
- If you have to try, you must be stupid.
- Don't try too hard; that way you've got an excuse if things go wrong.
- No pain, no pain!

Growth mindset

Beliefs

- Intelligence and ability can grow.
- Nurture determines intelligence and ability.
- If I apply myself more, seek help, take risks, change my strategy, then I've got a good chance of learning anything and thus growing my intelligence and talents.

Priority

- Improve myself.
- Learn through challenge, as this will help me to grow my talents.
- Seek interesting challenges that will stretch me and help me to learn

Attitude to challenging learning

- Challenge will help me learn.
- Difficulties are an inevitable part of the learning process.
- Failure means I need to adapt my strategies.

I apply myself when there is . . .

- An opportunity to learn new insights or skills.
- Enough challenge to stretch me.
- An opportunity to try something new.

Response to challenge

- There is no blame – I just want to know how to do it better next time.
- Feel inspired to have a go.
- Try various problem-solving strategies.
- Seek advice, support or new strategies.

Mottos

- Success comes with application.
- No matter how good you are at something, you can always improve.
- If you have to try, you must be learning.
- Always try hard; that way you've more chance of more success.
- No pain, no gain!

The challenge of mindsets

We need to be nurturing a growth mindset in ourselves, our colleagues and in every one of our pupils. The world is changing at a greater pace, with more knowledge, more professions and more options for communication and social networking than at any other time in history. Without a growth mindset, many young people will risk being left behind. 'The only person who is educated is the one who has learned how to learn – and change.'(Carl Rogers)[50]

If we want all our pupils to apply themselves today, there needs to be differing levels of challenge in our lessons, particularly because those with a fixed mindset will be more motivated by low levels of challenge.

Paradoxically, there is often a lack of correlation between mindset and performance in school; pupils with fixed mindsets seem to do just as well as pupils with growth mindsets. This is almost certainly to do with a lack of real challenge in school, particularly for the so-called 'gifted and talented' pupils who achieve the highest grades without significant effort or risk-taking. The problem of mindset in these pupils only really rears its head at university or in the workplace when difficulties are encountered, perhaps for the first time.

> You might think that students who were highly skilled would be the ones who relish a challenge and persevere in the face of setbacks. Instead, many of these students are the most worried about failure and the most likely to question their ability and to wilt when they hit obstacles.
>
> (Carol Dweck, 2000)[51]

Notes on mindsets

Nicholls and Miller[52] found four relatively distinct levels of reasoning among children about how ability and effort are differentiated:

Level 1 (apparent in 5 and 6 year olds)

Did not clearly differentiate in terms of cause and effect, the relationship between effort, ability and performance.

Level 2 (apparent in 7–9 year olds)

Viewed effort as the primary cause of performance outcomes, although effort and ability were not clearly differentiated in their thinking.

Level 3 (apparent in 9–12 year olds)

Began to differentiate ability and effort as causes of outcomes but did not always apply this distinction.

Level 4 (apparent in 10–13 year olds)

Clearly conceived that, although success requires a great deal of effort, one's ability can limit the effects additional effort can have on performance.

The fixed–growth split

According to Dweck, roughly half of us have a fixed mindset, and the other half, a growth mindset. Approximately 15 per cent of us straddle these groups, for example, by holding a fixed view about our maths ability but believing we can 'grow' our swimming skills.

Mindsets: the way forward

Developing a growth mindset in pupils and so enabling them to become lifelong learners involves doing all that has been suggested thus far, including:

- focusing lessons on the development of attitudes and skills, as well as knowledge;
- setting learning-related goals that necessitate pupils making progress to reach them;
- increasing steadily the amount of challenge we offer to pupils but supporting them when they falter;
- ensuring feedback identifies progress made and recommends the next steps;
- growing talents and gifts in every pupil, rather than seeking to identify the 'haves' and 'have nots';
- getting praise right (see pages 100–107);
- modelling growth-mindset behaviour ourselves.

Final quotes linked with application

The three great essentials to achieve anything worthwhile are, first, hard work; second, stick-to-itiveness; third, common sense.

(Thomas Edison, 1847–1931)

You think you're too small to make a difference? Then you've obviously never slept in the same room as a mosquito.

(African proverb)

Our deepest fear is not that we are inadequate. Our deepest fear is that we are powerful beyond measure. It is our light, not our darkness that frightens us most. We ask ourselves, 'Who am I to be brilliant, gorgeous, talented, and famous?' Actually, who are you not to be?

(Marianne Williamson, 1975)

Great sport is about reaction under pressure. Everything else is just exercise.

(Anon)

It's not that I'm so smart, it's just that I stay with problems longer.

(Albert Einstein, 1879–1955)

Before you become too entranced with gorgeous gadgets and mesmerizing video displays, let me remind you that information is not knowledge, knowledge is not wisdom, and wisdom is not foresight. Each grows out of the other, and we need them all.

(Arthur C. Clarke, 1917–2008)

The miracle, or the power, that elevates the few is to be found in their industry, application, and perseverance under the prompting of a brave, determined spirit.

(Mark Twain, 1835–1910)

Top 10 FACTS for application

1 Use a variety of strategies to increase pupils' desire to learn

Pupils' application will be determined by how much they value a learning goal, multiplied by how much they expect to achieve that goal; if desire is zero, then application will very likely also be zero.

2 Use the curriculum as a context for learning how to learn

In a rapidly changing world, one thing is certain: things will change. So, no matter how irrelevant some parts of the curriculum appear, they are still useful contexts within which to learn how to learn.

3 Identify learning-related goals

'Achievement is more likely to be increased when students invoke learning rather than performance strategies, accept rather than discount feedback, and benchmark to difficult rather than easy goals.' (John Hattie, 2009)[53]

4 Teach attitudes, as well as skills and knowledge

Outstanding learners have positive attitudes, are skilful in a number of aspects of learning and are able to access the information they need to complete any given task. Therefore, to grow into being an expert learner, pupils need to develop in all of the three domains of ASK (attitudes, skills and knowledge).

5 Preview learning

Previewing topics allows teachers to better understand pupils' prior knowledge and their levels of interest; it also allows pupils to prepare in their own time, thus increasing the chances of them being intentional learners in the next lesson.

6 Review learning in terms of attitudes, skills and knowledge

Broaden the criteria for awards and praise to include particular references to pupils developing learning attitudes, such as open-mindedness, curiosity, perseverance and willingness to try new strategies – as well as abilities such as reason-giving, supporting others and enhancing any of the skills of learning.

7 Encourage an openness to learning and risk-taking

'The willingness to invest in learning, to gain a reputation as a learner, and to show openness to experiences are the key dispositional factors that relate to achievement.' (John Hattie, 2009)[54]

8 Grow the gifts and talents of every pupil

Dweck's theory of fixed and growth mindsets[55] recognises that every pupil, not just the talented few, can develop their intelligence and talents through application, strategy, risk-taking and support.

9 Create rich feedback cultures

Feedback that helps pupils better understand their learning goals, their position in relation to these goals and the steps that are needed next will have a powerful effect on learning progress and achievement.

10 Model growth mindsets

All of these recommendations will be more authentic if teachers model growth mindset behaviours such as tenacity, accepting fallibility, taking risks and setting themselves learning-related targets.

4

Challenge

FEEDBACK
APPLICATION
CHALLENGE
THINKING
SELF-ESTEEM

'We need more challenge and less instruction, since it is from challenge that one grows in body, mind and spirit.'

(Matthew Lipman, 1991)[56]

Challenge: 'one ring to rule them all'

The notion of 'challenge' is central to this book. It underpins each of the other four FACTS in the following ways:

Challenge and feedback

The greater the challenge, the higher the probability that pupils will seek and need feedback. Challenge has been shown to influence pupil learning and achievement in powerful ways.

Challenge and application

If pupils have a growth mindset, they will tend to appreciate tasks that are challenging. Conversely, challenge is the key factor which, if increased bit by bit over time, will help those with a fixed mindset to develop their own growth mindset and, therefore, a greater desire for meaningful learning.

Challenge and thinking

As I will show in the next chapter, when pupils are challenged, they will think more, and they will use more reasoning, inquiry and creativity in a bid to seek better answers to problems. In this way, challenge is a prerequisite for anything other than superficial thinking.

Challenge and self-esteem

Lastly, as I will show in the final section of FACTS, self-esteem is about achieving a balance between pupils knowing they can succeed while at the same time believing they can cope with difficulties. In this way, then, challenge is a vital ingredient in the development of meaningful self-esteem.

What is challenge?

Challenge makes a situation more demanding or stimulating and is used to encourage pupils to learn more than they otherwise would.

Referring to Figure 4.1, here is a further explanation:

Let's say, for example, that when 3-year-old Susan concentrates, she is able to ride a three-wheeled tricycle confidently. This is her current ability (CA), represented by the middle line on the diagram. Eventually, riding a tricycle will be an almost automatic action for Susan because she no longer needs to concentrate on pedalling and steering. This is her subconscious ability (SA), represented by the lower line on the diagram. So now, whenever Susan rides a tricycle she is in the PRACTICE zone because she is consolidating an existing skill (the ability to ride a tricycle) rather than learning a new one.

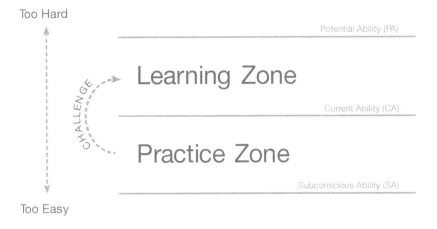

FIGURE 4.1 Identifying challenge

Once Susan is fully competent at riding her tricycle, she will be ready to progress to a two-wheeled bicycle. This is when the upper line on the graph becomes relevant because it represents the upper limit of what Susan might be able to achieve with support and encouragement. On the graph, I refer to this as her potential ability (PA), which would be riding a bicycle with encouragement. Now whenever she tries this new activity, Susan will be in the LEARNING zone.

The reason I have chosen cycling as an example is to draw attention to the characteristics of the learning zone: wobbling, feeling unsure and perhaps even wondering whether you'll ever succeed. Not only is this what happens when a child learns to ride a bike, it is also typical of other types of learning. Of course, most learning doesn't involve a literal wobble, but it does involve a cognitive wobble. Ask any layman and he'll call it getting 'outside his comfort zone' and then go on to mention similar characteristics: uncertainty, nervousness and wobble.

Challenge in this context then is concerned with encouraging pupils (and ourselves) into the learning zone. These ideas are built on the work of Soviet psychologist, Lev Vygotsky (see page 58).

The teaching target model

Of course, there is a time to challenge and a time to support. We would not want our pupils to work only within the learning zone, as this would reduce their self-confidence. Nor would we want pupils to spend the majority of their time in the practice zone, as this would slow their rate of progress. The optimum would look something like Figure 4.2, with a balance between learning zone and practice zone activities.

I've called this the TTM because it helps to identify where we should focus our teaching. Consider the following lesson scenarios:

■ Some pupils are struggling even to begin the task. In this case, they are probably beyond their PA and are now in the 'Too Hard Zone'. They therefore need some support to move into the learning zone.

■ Your pupils have made a good start with a task but encounter some problems that prevent them from completing it. Great! Encourage them to keep going and praise them for their determination because they are almost certainly in the learning zone.

■ Your pupils are completing tasks easily. They are probably then in the practice zone, so should be encouraged into the learning zone with either 'Scaffolders' or 'Wobblers' (see page 59).

■ A few pupils are bored by the task (and perhaps beginning to disrupt others). This is a strong indication that they are in the 'Too Easy Zone', and so need a lot more challenge.

Please note that a key aspect of the TTM is balance. Notice that the 'progress wave' begins in the practice zone, then moves into the learning zone and then

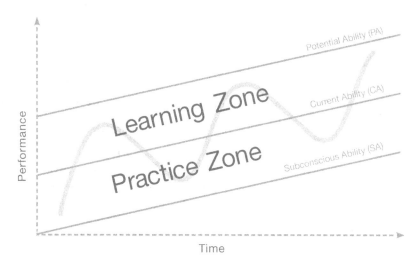

FIGURE 4.2 The Teaching Target model

back to the practice zone. This is deliberate; lessons should normally begin by connecting with prior understanding, extending that understanding through challenge and then consolidating the new attitudes, skills or knowledge.

In support of the teaching target model

The teaching target model is powerful for the following reasons:

1 The TTM focuses attention on potential ability

Eminent educational theorists Lev Vygotsky, Reuven Feuerstein and Carol Dweck, among others, have all drawn attention to the greater significance of PA compared with current ability.

Lev Vygotsky focused his attention on what a child will be able to do. He believed that learning leads to development. In contrast, Piaget believed that development leads to learning. For these reasons, Vygotsky was more concerned with the upper limit of a child's ZPD (see 'In the "zone" with Lev Vygotsky' on page 58).

Reuven Feuerstein, a student of Carl Jung and Jean Piaget, based his programme of instrumental enrichment on the importance of learning potential. Founded on the premise that intelligence is not a fixed quality determined by genes but a quality that can be modified, instrumental enrichment identifies what a child is capable of learning. In the BBC's *Transformers* series, Feuerstein remarked how frustrated he was that education systems throughout the world tend to focus on children's abilities (line CA on the TTM) rather than on what they might be capable of with support (line PA on the TTM). Like Vygotsky, he was critical of IQ tests and sought to discover the most significant barriers preventing children from reaching their potential.

Carol Dweck's theory of fixed and growth mindsets also supports the focus on potential rather than current ability, as explained on pages 45–47.

2 The TTM challenges our understanding of learning

Learning involves 'wobble' as a response to difficulty. When we reflect on this, we assess classroom activities for their learning potential, or lack of it. For example, how often do we assume that when pupils encounter new information they must be learning?

I was struck by this recently when observing two lessons in a middle school. The Year 5s were beginning a topic on the water cycle in science and the Year 7s were looking at rivers in geography. The teacher in each case presented a diagram to introduce the topic, labelling it with terms such as transpiration, evaporation, floodplain, tributary and so on. In both classes, the pupils, who were focused and engaged, were asked to recreate the diagrams in their books and, in both cases, the teacher circulated around the room praising the pupils who were doing well and supporting those who struggled. Each lesson finished with a review of the new information in pairs and then as a whole class. Structurally it was a 'good lesson'.

Though both of these lessons seemed to engage the pupils, I wondered how much wobble there was and in which zone most of the pupils spent their time.

I was most concerned about those pupils who were completing the task easily because to me this was a sign that they were not struggling and therefore not in the learning zone (and yet were being praised for it).

I realise that many of us will assume that because the pupils were encountering new information, they were therefore learning. However, the problem with such a conclusion is that, for many pupils, it is not much of a challenge to listen, watch and then repeat. For example, whenever I read a picture book at bedtime to my 3-year-old daughter, she will very often take the book out of my hands and 'read' it back to me, even if it's the first time she's come across the book. Of course, she's not word perfect but generally she doesn't seem to struggle to remember and repeat new information. So how much of a challenge is it likely to be for many of the 10 and 12 year olds in the lessons mentioned above to remember and repeat? On pages 56–57 I explore what could have been done to challenge these pupils more.

Using the teaching target model

Achieving a balance between learning zone and practice zone activities is the goal of the TTM. It is not easy to achieve. In fact, with thirty pupils of varying ASK in one class, it is perhaps impossible to strike a perfect balance. Nevertheless, it is a worthy goal.

1 Connect

To use the model, start your lesson by connecting to pupils' prior learning so they begin in the practice zone. All the lesson ideas at the back of this book are designed to do this by identifying familiar key concepts. Then, after a short exploration of what they already know, use some of the challenge techniques that follow to encourage your pupils into their learning zone.

2 Identify

The next thing to focus on is pupils' PA. A useful rule of thumb for this is to seek the point at which pupils begin to fail, then ease back slightly. This contrasts with the negative perceptions of 'hot housing' or pushing pupils to achieve what you want them to achieve while disregarding the building blocks that reveal themselves when the children experience difficulty.

A good example of this easing-back strategy comes from a P4C lesson with a group of 6-year-olds in Masterton, New Zealand. The question they had chosen was, 'Who did the old lady sell her animals to?' I encouraged them to focus on the concept of 'selling' by asking them a series of questions. They responded reasonably well until I asked: 'Could I sell you an idea?' At that point, their faces were blank. However, instead of giving up that line of inquiry, I merely eased back slightly by asking: 'Could I sell you a joke?' This then gave them a hook for wondering whether abstract things such as jokes, smells and dreams could be bought and sold. Afterwards, the teachers of the children remarked how impressed they were with their pupils' ability to think about abstract ideas in such a reflective way.

This shows how, by using the TTM, you can identify and adjust an appropriate level of expectation. This has a major impact on pupil achievement. In fact, in 1968 and 1992, Rosenthal and Jacobson showed that if teachers expected enhanced performance from some children, the children did indeed show that enhancement. Describing this as the Pygmalion effect, the psychologists showed that raised expectancies can essentially affect reality by creating self-fulfilling prophecies.[57]

3 Challenge

There are two senses of the term 'challenge' conveyed in this book. The first is to do with wobbling, and the second with scaffolding. Both perform essentially the same function of encouraging pupils to move from practice to learning (represented by the challenge arrow in Figure 4.1). However, they do so in different ways.

Challenge as wobble

The examples used thus far in this chapter are concerned with creating cognitive wobble. There are a number of techniques that you can use for this, many of which are described on page 59. In the middle-school lessons described on pages 56–57, the following wobble strategies could be used alongside the practical activity of redrawing the relevant diagram.

Year 5 lesson about the water cycle. Those pupils who are finding it an easy enough task to recreate the diagram in their books could be asked, for example, where the energy for the whole process comes from. When they answer 'the sun' (for that is what they were told in the teacher's introduction), they could be challenged to think of why the water cycle still works north of the Arctic Circle during the three winter months in which the sun never rises.

Year 7 lesson about rivers. Similarly, the pupils who are finding the redrawing and labelling of 'a river from source to mouth' straightforward could be asked where the best place to build a house would be (remembering that the flattest part – the flood plain – is also the wettest place).

Challenge as 'scaffolding'

Though the term is often attributed to Lev Vygotsky (1896–1934), the metaphor 'scaffolding' was first used by Jerome Bruner in 1976[58] to explore the nature of support an adult might offer a child to help them progress from current to potential achievement. It is a useful term to use when considering Vygotsky's ZPD since the ZPD represents the gap between these two positions: what a child can achieve by themselves when focused (CA in Figure 4.1), and what they can achieve in collaboration with others (PA in Figure 4.1).

Of course, there are many other types of challenge which, if present, may make the use of wobblers or scaffolders unnecessary, including:

- **Task-based challenge**. For example: 'make all the numbers between 0 and 15 using only 2, 7, _ ÷ ± ( ) '
- **Social challenge**. Helping pupils find the right balance between conforming at school and being creative.
- **Scholarly challenge**. For example: the teaching and learning of successful exam techniques or the structure of an essay.

'Give it here, I'll do it for you!'

4 Support

Two main obstacles to achieving the optimum balance between practice and learning are:

■ Teachers very often attempt to design the wobble out of lessons or at least try to rescue pupils when they are wobbling.

■ Pupils often feel like giving up when the going gets tough.

Both these situations should be tackled so that as many lessons as possible reflect the progress spirals in Figure 4.2 in which pupils begin in their practice zone, move into their learning zone for a period of time, then consolidate their new learning back in the practice zone.

Of course, taking pupils beyond their PA should be avoided, as this is likely to lead to disengagement and behaviour problems. This also happens when teachers rush to their pupils' aid and help them to such an extent that the challenge is removed. This should also be avoided. A far better approach is to support pupils just enough so they can engage with the task in their own learning zone.

In the 'zone' with Lev Vygotsky

Lev Vygotsky was an innovative Soviet psychologist whose ideas have received great attention from all those concerned with the intellectual development of children.

Vygotsky was one of the first critics of IQ and the view that intellectual capacity is 'fixed'. His famous theory of the Zone of Proximal Development[59] presents an alternative view and one that is relevant to the ideas presented in this book. He contrasts two levels of intellectual development. He identifies the cognitive capacities that:

■ are fully developed at a particular time

■ are in the process of being developed.

This second kind of development is dependent on a cooperative interaction between children and adults, children and more able children or, indeed, between children and cultural artefacts such as stories. The growth that is possible in this field of cooperation is called the ZPD.

This ZPD is represented by the learning zone in the TTM. It is also exactly where the 'challenge', as explained in this book, seeks to operate. The challenging teacher explores with the children, usually through dialogue, what they might be able to understand with help that they cannot necessarily understand at the present time. And, although they may struggle, the struggle itself leads them to strengthen attitudes, develop skills and acquire knowledge that they can use in coping with future challenges.

Vygotsky's theories also underpin the growth mindset (because cognitive capacities can be modified) and justify an emphasis on challenge in teaching and learning.

Types of challenge

I suggest three types of challenge you can apply in lessons so that pupils will struggle a little more but benefit through their struggles. They are:

Wobblers

These are techniques designed to create 'cognitive conflict' in the minds of pupils, which will, in turn, lead to deeper thinking and longer-lasting learning. Cognitive conflict is explored in depth in the chapter on Thinking (see pages 77–96).

Scaffolders

These are primarily open-questioning techniques designed to stretch, while at the same time support, pupils' thinking. They are mainly Socratic questions (after Socrates the ancient Greek, famous for asking searching questions about such essential concepts as courage, beauty and a good life).

Concept stretchers

These are techniques designed to broaden pupils' understanding, application and repertoire of the generalised ideas we call concepts. Most of the lesson plans in this book have at least one concept-stretching exercise within them, with many more available from www.p4c.com.

Over the following pages, I have put together a guide to these three types of challenge. They are by no means the only types; they might not even be the best. However, not only have they worked very well for me over the years, but they also form the bedrock for the challenging learning model explored in Chapter 7 and the lesson plans beginning on page 127. So they are worth considering.

Wobblers

Wobblers aim to create cognitive conflict (see page 59 for a full explanation) in the minds of pupils by challenging their initial thoughts, making them question their assumptions and offering alternative perspectives they may not have considered. Here's an example:

TEACHER:	What is history?
ADAM:	Stuff that happened in the past.
TEACHER:	So your breakfast is history?
ADAM:	Yes.
SUSAN:	But we're not going to study what Adam had for breakfast, are we?
TEACHER:	Why does it make a difference whether we study it or not?
RACHEL:	Because that's what history is about – studying things that happened in the past.
TEACHER:	So if we were to study Adam's breakfast, then we'd be doing history, would we?
RACHEL:	I guess so, though why would we study that? That's boring.
TEACHER:	But we study what past civilisations have eaten, don't we? For example, what the Romans ate during their orgies.
TAS:	Yes, but the Romans are important. Adam's not important.
ADAM:	Thanks very much!
TAS:	You know what I mean. The Romans had a big impact on our lives whereas Adam hasn't yet.
ANITA:	So maybe history is studying important things from the past?
TEACHER:	But if the events are not in the past, are they not history?
ELLIE:	Of course they wouldn't be history, they'd be the present.
TEACHER:	But did anyone watch the airplanes flying into the twin towers in New York and think 'This is history in the making'?
SAM:	But that was still the past because there was a time delay between it happening and the pictures being shown on our TVs.
MOHAMMED:	But that would mean everything that is shown on the news is history, wouldn't it?
TEACHER:	Indeed! So, history is actually everything we see and hear since there is a delay, however slight, between the event actually happening and us seeing it!

Wobbler 1: if A=B

This is a process of asking what a concept means, taking whatever the pupil says and then testing it by turning it around and adding an example. For example, from the dialogue above:

TEACHER:	What is history?
ADAM:	Stuff that happened in the past?
TEACHER:	Does that mean stuff that happened in the past is history? For example, your breakfast?

This structure can be represented as: If A=B then does B=A? A is the concept that you are considering, in this case 'history'. B is the pupils' response, in this case 'stuff that happened in the past'. To challenge the pupils' answers in the example, we applied the structure: If A=B, then does B=A?

Adam's Breakfast

Some examples of wobbler 1

If a friend (A) is someone I trust (B), then is someone I trust (B) a friend (A)? For example, I trust a nurse to help me when I'm sick, does that mean she's my friend?

If a holiday (A) is taking a break (B) then if I take a break (B), am I on holiday (A)? For example, is my tea break or my half-hour game of chess a holiday?

If bullying (A) means hurting someone (B), does that mean that if I hurt someone (B) I'm bullying (A) them? For example, what if I foul someone in a football match? Or give someone some bad news?

If a hero (A) is someone who is brave (B), does that mean a brave (B) person is a hero (A)? For example, a shy pupil asks a question in class. They may be brave but are they are a hero?

Wobbler 2: NOT A

An alternative to the first wobbler is simply to add a negative. In the example dialogue, this happened as follows:

ANITA: So maybe history is studying important things from the past?
TEACHER: But if the events are not in the past, are they not history?
ELLIE: Of course they wouldn't be history, they'd be the present.

The structure here is: If A=B, then if it's NOT B, is it also NOT A? A is the concept that you are considering, in this case 'history'. B is the pupil's response, in this case 'stuff that happened in the past'. So this time, to challenge the pupil's answer, we ask: '. . . does that mean if it does not happen in the past (B) that it's not history (A): for example, current affairs that are so profound that we feel we're watching history in the making?'

Some examples of wobbler 2

If a friend (A) is someone I trust (B), then is someone I don't trust (not B) not my friend (not A)? For example, if I don't trust a friend to pay back a loan, then are we no longer friends?

If a holiday (A) is going away somewhere (B) then if I don't go away (not B), am I not on holiday (not A)? For example, if I stay at home during the school holidays, am I not on holiday?

If bullying (A) means hurting someone (B), then if I don't hurt someone (not B) am I not bullying (not A) them? For example, if I don't hit them but instead encourage everyone to ignore them, am I not bullying?

If a hero (A) is someone I respect (B), does that mean that if I don't respect (not B) them they are not a hero (not A)? For example, the apartheid government in South Africa didn't respect Nelson Mandela for years, but to millions around the world he was (and still is) a hero.

Wobbler 3: general to specific

You may need to move between generalisations and specific examples to make the first two handy hints work, particularly with the 'Not A' version. For example, if you were to ask what a friend is and your pupils replied 'someone who is nice', it would seem strange then to ask 'does that mean someone who is not nice is not your friend?' The answer must surely be yes!

However, if you were to move from the general to the specific, this handy hint will still work and give you more food for thought. For example:

TEACHER: What is a friend?
PUPIL: Someone who is nice.
TEACHER: Do friends always have to be nice to each other? For example, what if your friend won't share their sweets with you today; does that mean you stop being friends?

This then gives you the opportunity to explore questions such as:

■ When is doing something that is not nice still compatible with friendship?

- Are there some 'not-nice' things that a friend might do which would actually be good for your friendship?
- Can you think of an example of something a friend did that wasn't very nice but that didn't threaten your friendship?

Wobbler 4: quantifying

This is a wobbler I don't get to use very often but when I do, it creates some productive dilemmas. To use the quantifying tactic, I simply ask pupils to put a figure to their woolly estimation.

For example:

PUPIL: A friend is someone you've known for a long time.
TEACHER: How much time?
PUPIL: I don't know, maybe a couple of years.
TEACHER: Blimey, does that mean I have to know someone for 2 years or more before we can be friends?
PUPIL: No, of course not. OK, well maybe a few weeks are enough!
TEACHER: So, if I've known someone for a few weeks, will I automatically become friends with them?

'Two years from now, when the clock strikes twelve then I'll be your friend'

Wobbler notes

Sticking to the advice in the following four suggestions will improve the success rate of all the wobblers you might use:

1 Wobbling, not point-scoring

As you may have noted, these techniques lie comfortably in the Socratic tradition. Socrates (469–399 BC) often posed a series of questions to help a person reflect on their underlying beliefs and the extent of their knowledge. Such questioning is not about point-scoring or proving someone wrong. Indeed, it is said of Socrates that he questioned his fellow Athenians not through an arrogant sense of his being right and them being wrong but through a desire to unearth contradictions and misconceptions that were blocking the way to true inquiry.

And so it is with these wobblers: they are not designed to prove pupils wrong. Rather, they are tools to help them go beyond the easy answer or first response, to identify contradictions and misconceptions and, ultimately, to form the habit of questioning their own ideas.

2 Humour and humility

Humour and humility were difficult to convey in the example dialogues, but they are key characteristics of the wobbler approach. Putting pupils on the spot in an attempt to discredit or disprove their hypotheses would be arrogant and discouraging for them. However, it seems to be far more productive if we laugh with the pupils (rather than at them) and admit we don't know what the concept means any more than the pupils do. This helps establish an expectation of co-inquiry with the teacher rather than a dependence on the teacher's authority and an anxiety about getting the answers wrong.

3 A little bit of trickery

With humour and humility still in mind, the wobbler challenge could be said to be a form of trickery. Of course, trickery has negative connotations such as the trickery of a conman. This is partly why it's worth mentioning that with these wobblers I am promoting a trickery that is positive, fun and engaging for pupils. It is also worth mentioning because the Latin root word for challenge is 'calumnia', meaning trickery.

4 Drawing out rather than stuffng in

A more commonly known word origin, this time of 'education', is from the Latin word 'educere' meaning 'to lead or draw out'.

Wobblers attempt to do just that. Rather than giving pupils the answers, the ideas, the facts or the definitions, wobblers all strive to tease out pupils' ideas. Once 'out' they can be examined, played with, cross-referenced and, of course, challenged.

'Drawing out' . . . NOT 'Stuffing in'

A major purpose of education is to cultivate open-mindedness and intelligence.

Defined in terms of the aptitude for acquiring knowledge, intelligence depends upon an alert curiosity. The cultivation of intelligence depends on freedom to exercise curiosity.

(Jiddu Krishnamurti, 1895–1986, described by the Dalai Lama as one of the greatest thinkers of the age)

Scaffolders

Scaffolders are questions designed to draw out from pupils what they know and might know, as well as to encourage them to question their own thinking.

I have called them scaffolders because they are intended to support and encourage pupils when they are in the learning zone, as opposed to wobblers, which aim to get pupils into the zone via cognitive conflict.

The first scaffolders' framework (page 67) is based on Bloom's taxonomy. Though some critics have questioned the sequential, hierarchical nature of Bloom's taxonomy, it remains one of the best-known and oft-referred-to schemas for thinking. Please note, however, there is a challenge to Bloom's taxonomy in the Thinking chapter on page 78.

'He who is afraid to ask is ashamed of learning.'

(Danish proverb)

The next framework is based, like wobblers, on the Socratic tradition, although these questions, in contrast to wobblers, are designed to seek clarity rather than to confuse pupils. This second set of questions is categorised using the mnemonic CRAVE, which stands for:

Clarification
Reasons
Assumptions
Viewpoints
Effects
Questions about questions.

Question time

According to research published in 1986 by Mary Budd Rowe at the Department of Childhood Education, University of Florida, teachers do not give enough thinking time after asking a question.[61]

Analysis of over 300 classroom recordings showed:

- When teachers ask a question they wait 1 second or less for pupils to begin an answer.

- If the reply does not start in 1 second the teacher repeats or rephrases the question or calls on someone else.

- After a pupil replies, teachers typically react or go on with more questioning in less than 1 second; there is little chance for second thoughts by pupils.

- Teachers give the more able pupils more time to answer than they give the less able pupils.

When teachers increased the average wait time to 3 seconds, Rowe and her team found:

1   The length of explanations among advantaged groups increased fivefold, and among disadvantaged groups, sevenfold.

2   The number of unsolicited but appropriate comments increased dramatically.

3   Failures to respond decreased from an average of 30 per cent to less than 5 per cent.

4   The number of questions asked by children rose sharply.

Further studies from the same team recommended that the classroom be conceptualised as a two-player game in which the quality of inquiry will tend to improve when there is a better equity in the distribution of moves (where the teacher is one player and collectively the pupils are the second player).

Scaffolding framework 1: Bloom's taxonomy

Higher order

Evaluation

- Do you agree that . . . ?
- Which is the most important . . . ?
- What criteria would you use to assess . . . ?

Verbs: appraise, argue, assess, attach, choose, compare, defend, estimate, judge, predict, rate, score, select, support, value, evaluate.

Synthesis

- What would you predict/infer from . . . ?
- What might happen if you combined . . . ?
- Which solutions would you suggest for . . . ?

Verbs: arrange, assemble, collect, compose, construct, create, design, develop, formulate, manage, organise, plan, prepare, propose, set up, write.

Analysis

- What are the parts or features of . . . ?
- How does . . . compare/contrast with . . . ?
- What evidence can you list for . . . ?

Verbs: analyse, appraise, calculate, categorise, compare, contrast, criticise, differentiate, discriminate, distinguish, examine, experiment, question, test.

Lower order

Application

- How is . . . an example of . . . ?
- How is . . . related to . . . ?
- Why is . . . significant?

Verbs: apply, choose, demonstrate, dramatise, employ, illustrate, interpret, operate, practise, schedule, sketch, solve, use, write.

Comprehension

- How could you write eighteen per cent numerically?
- What was the moral of the story?
- What does 'Je m'appelle James' mean?

Verbs: classify, describe, discuss, explain, express, identify, indicate, locate, recognise, report, restate, review.

Knowledge

- What is a ... ?
- When did ... happen?
- Where are the ... ?

Verbs: arrange, define, duplicate, label, list, memorise, name, order, recognise, relate, recall, repeat, reproduce, state.

These questions are categorised according to the Taxonomy of Educational Objectives (Cognitive Domain) by Benjamin Bloom[60] though please refer to page 78 for a critique of Bloom's work.

Scaffolding framework 2: Socratic questions

C – Clarification

Basic 'tell me more' questions that invite pupils to 'go deeper'.

- Why are you saying that?
- What exactly does this mean?
- How does this relate to what we have been talking about?
- What do we already know about this?
- Can you give me an example?
- Are you saying ... or ... ?
- Can you rephrase that, please?

R – Reasons

Checking that reasons given by pupils actually do support the conclusions they are drawing.

- Can you give me an example of that?
- Are these reasons good enough?
- How might it be refuted?

- How can I be sure of what you are saying?
- Why is . . . happening?
- What evidence is there to support what you are saying?
- On what authority are you basing your argument?

A – Assumptions

Asking pupils to think about the presuppositions and unquestioned beliefs upon which they are founding their arguments.

- What are you taking for granted?
- Are you assuming that . . . ?
- Please explain why/how . . . ?
- How can you verify or disprove that assumption?
- What would happen if . . . ?
- Do you agree or disagree with . . . ?
- Aren't you thinking that . . . ?

V – Viewpoints

Most arguments are given from particular viewpoints. Seek alternatives from your pupils.

- What alternative ways of looking at this are there?
- Why is . . . necessary?
- Who benefits from this?
- Why is it better than . . . ?
- What are the strengths and weaknesses of . . . ?
- How are . . . and . . . similar?
- How could you look at this in another way?

E – Effects

Arguments and ideas may have logical implications and consequences that can be forecast. These questions invite pupils to consider the possible effects or consequences of ideas or actions.

- What would happen then?
- Doesn't it follow that . . . ?
- What are the consequences of that assumption?
- How does . . . affect . . . ?

- How does . . . fit with what we learnt before?
- Are you suggesting that . . . ?
- What is the best . . . ? Why?

Q – Questions

Questions about questions (metacognition). These questions are designed to ask the pupils to reflect on the relative merits of their questions.

- How effective was your question?
- Which of your questions turned out to be the most useful?
- What was the point of asking that question?
- Why do you think I asked this question?
- What does that mean?
- Can you improve any of your/my questions?
- What would you do to improve your questions in future?

Intuition and concepts constitute . . . the elements of all our knowledge, so that neither concepts without intuition, nor intuition without concepts, can yield knowledge.

Immanuel Kant, German philosopher, 1724–1804

Concept stretchers

As you read through the forms of challenge I recommend, you will notice they all have one thing in common: a focus on key concepts. This is no coincidence; people's thoughts and actions reflect the complexity, richness, diversity and coherence of their concepts. If we are unable to make connections between our concepts then often more complex meanings escape us. In *Thinking in Education*, (2nd edn), Matthew Lipman says of concepts: 'When we cluster things in terms of their similarities, we are said to have a concept of them. . . concepts are the vehicles of thought, entities by which thought is carried on.'[62]

So concepts are not simply facts, information or data but something more fundamental than that. They are the very foundations of thinking.

On the resource site p4c.com, Steve Williams, Roger Sutcliffe and I have created exercises to explore and build pupils' conceptual understanding. We call the exercises 'concept stretchers' and have categorised them into different ways of exploring concepts, with:

- **comparisons** (establishing similarities and differences)
- **dialogues** (considering and constructing dialogues about a concept)
- **examples** (categorising persons/things, situations and utterances)

- **opinions** (agreeing and disagreeing with opinions)
- **questions** (reflecting on questions arising from a concept)

Of these, comparisons and examples will be covered here; the others are explored on www.p4c.com

Concept stretchers: comparisons

A common way of challenging pupils' perceptions of a concept is to draw comparisons with another. These comparisons often take the form of similarities and differences (connections and distinctions). For example, the similarities and differences between:

- **history** (the study) and **history** (the past)
- **music** and **noise**
- **thoughts** and **dreams**
- **speech** and **language**
- **friends** and **classmates**
- **shape** and **size**
- **a holiday** and **a weekend**
- **biodegradable** and **reusable**
- **a hero** and **a villain**
- **writing a creative story** and **telling a lie**
- **knowledge** and **wisdom**

In Figure 4.3, you can see the sorts of concepts that can be compared with the use of a Venn diagram. There are other examples over the next few pages. You can use other visual tools to help with these distinctions, including continuums, thinking circles, concept maps and so on.

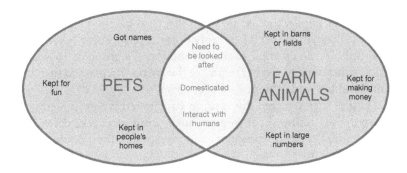

FIGURE 4.3 Using Venn diagrams to compare concepts

Other examples

1   Knowledge and wisdom
2   Thoughts and dreams
3   Secrets and lies
4   Friends and classmates
5   Tourists and travellers

Venn diagrams

Venn diagrams: hated by pupils in maths but great as a visual tool for thinking. And they work with even the youngest pupils. In fact, one of the best lessons I've seen in a long time was in a nursery class in Thornaby-on-Tees in the UK. The teacher asked her class of 4-year-olds to sit in a circle, around which she placed fifty objects. She then showed them a picture of a 4-year-old boy, asked them each to pick one of the objects that they thought belonged to the boy and to place it in a hoop that she laid on the floor alongside the boy's picture. As they did this, she asked them to give reasons why they thought, for example, the toothbrush that one of them had picked would belong to the boy.

Then she showed them a picture of a girl about the same age and asked them to do the same thing, only this time they were asked to place their chosen object into the hoop next to the girl's picture. The problem was, there were thirty children in the class and they had begun with fifty objects, thirty of which were already in the boy's hoop. So she asked the ten children who didn't have an object to think of a solution to their problem. Of course, they suggested moving some of the objects from the boy's hoop into the girl's hoop which they proceeded to do until the teacher asked the other children to challenge this if they so wished.

The children eventually decided that some objects could belong to boys and girls, at which point the teacher introduced a third hoop and laid it next to a picture showing a boy and a girl. The lesson finished with the children negotiating (by giving reasons, listening to each other and then making decisions) which objects should go in which hoop. What I thought was the stroke of genius was the introduction of the third hoop rather than going for the abstract notion of overlapping hoops.

With older pupils, the use of Venn diagrams can be extended by asking them to alter the diagram so that it best represents the relationship between two (or more) concepts. I used an example of this recently with a group of 16-year-olds studying physical education. At the beginning of the lesson, I remarked that 'sport' and 'war' are one and the same thing.

Of course they rejected this idea, so I suggested we use a Venn diagram to test my hypothesis, asking them to place such terms as attack, defend, bravery, rules of engagement, take no prisoners and any others they could think of into the following diagram:

The more of these terms they placed into category 2, the more I gloated that my hypothesis was right. This of course made them more determined to prove

FIGURE 4.4 Using Venn diagrams with young children

me wrong and to find terms that would go in areas 1, 3 and 4. I then challenged them to decide which of the following diagrams represented the actual relationship between sport and war (Figure 4.5 being the original diagram):

Extension: I asked some groups to add a third circle to represent 'games'.

More examples of Venn diagrams can be found on pages 123, 142, 155 and 179 (lesson plans) and on www.p4c.com.

A variation on Venn diagrams can be found in the work of Matthew Lipman and Ann Sharp. They don't give the tool a name, so I have called it 'concentric circles'.

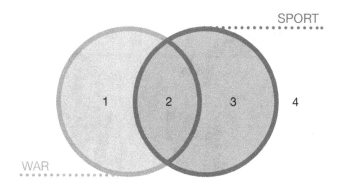

FIGURE 4.5 Sport and war

Diagram 2
All Sport is War

Diagram 3
All War is Sport

Diagram 4
Sport and War are separate

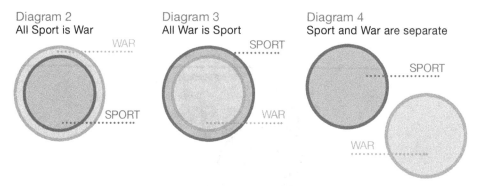

FIGURE 4.6 Sport and war versions

A variation on Venn diagrams can be found in the work of Matthew Lipman and Ann Sharp. They don't give the tool a name, so I have called it 'Concentric circles'

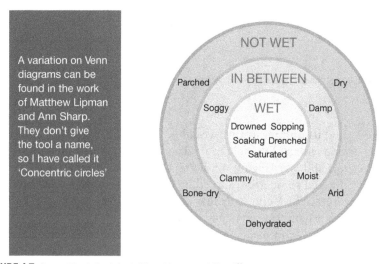

FIGURE 4.7 Concentric circles (adapted from Lipman and Sharp)[63]

Concept stretchers: examples

One effective approach to exploring concepts is to generate possible examples of a given concept and write them down for the pupils to ponder. The list might include items you think are good examples of the concept, as well as those that might be contrary items and borderline cases. For example, taking the concept of 'courage' (from the concept stretchers database on www.p4c.com), courage might involve:

Good examples:

1   Standing up to a bully.
2   Risking embarrassment in order to try out something you think is worthwhile.

Contrary examples:

1   Putting the blame on to someone else when you have done something wrong because you are afraid to be blamed or punished.
2   Not doing something you really want to do because you fear you might feel embarrassed.

Borderline cases:

1   Being extremely shy and not being able to get over it.
2   Overcoming shyness and embarrassment by taking a pill.
3   Stopping someone from bullying another person. You are a lot stronger than both of them.

Top 10 FACTS for challenge

1 Challenge is necessary

Without challenge, progress will be slowed and pupils will be less fit for learning. As Churchill once said: 'Kites rise against the wind, not with it'.

2 Challenge should make pupils wobble

The aim of challenge is to take pupils out of their comfort zone and into their learning zone, where they will think more, focus more and wobble more – all of which are signs of deep learning.

3 Benchmark to challenging goals

Learning intentions and success criteria should identify goals that are so challenging they may not be achieved within a lesson, and certainly not without hard work and persistence.

4 Create cognitive conflict

Challenge is not just about extending goals; it is also about throwing obstacles in the way of learners, creating counter-arguments and deliberately generating cognitive dissonance in pupils' minds.

5 Challenge with humility and good humour

It is more productive to laugh with pupils rather than at them and for teachers to admit that they don't know the answer. This helps establish an expectation of co-inquiry with the teacher rather than a dependence on the teacher's authority, accompanied by an anxiety about getting the answers wrong.

6 Challenge should be differentiated

The ZPD (the difference between 'present' and 'potential' levels of development) is different for each pupil. Therefore, scaffolding techniques such as questioning should be carefully tailored to help each pupil work within their own ZPD.

7 Challenge as part of a community of inquiry

Though challenge needs to be differentiated, it is also less threatening when encountered as part of a group. Conventions such as the community of inquiry are ideal for addressing these concerns.

8 Increase thinking time after asking challenging questions

Mary Budd Rowe (1986) found that by increasing the thinking time after a question has been asked, to 3 seconds, dramatic improvements in the quality and quantity of pupils' answers were recorded.[64]

9 In the long term, challenge will improve self-esteem and motivation

Many teachers worry about challenging pupils too much for fear of demotivating them or harming their self-esteem. Actually, the opposite effect is usually noted: the more pupils get used to challenge, the more they enjoy it and believe they can deal with it – thus increasing self-esteem and motivation.

10 Challenge links feedback, application, thinking and self-esteem

In a sense, challenge is the central theme to all learning because, without challenge there is no need for feedback, and without feedback (from oneself as well as from others) there is very little reflective thought or any real sense of achievement.

5 Thinking

FEEDBACK
APPLICATION
CHALLENGE
THINKING
SELF-ESTEEM

'The school should always have as its aim that the young man leaves it as a harmonious personality, not as a specialist. The development of general ability for independent thinking and judgement should always be placed foremost.'

(Albert Einstein, 1950)[65]

Albert Einstein

Why teach thinking?

As I watch my daughter grow, I am fascinated to see how she learns to think. After just a few months, she seemed to deliberately compare one object with another by studying each one in turn through sight, sound or, more often, taste. By the time she was 11 months old, she was thinking of alternative ways to give food to our dog, Hector. We'd tell her not to give her finger-food to the dog, so she'd smile at us, put the food behind her back and waggle it for the dog to take. By the age of 2 she was reasoning with us: 'Not go to my bed, go to Mummy, Daddy's bed. I go to my bed, I'll cry'.

This was an almost nightly argument for a week or two. My daughter's natural development of thinking provokes a question: since she has already learnt how to think, does she really need to be taught how to do it in school?

To answer this, it is important to distinguish between types of thinking which, to my mind, consist of two main categories: routine and reflective.

Routine thinking would include the thinking we do almost subconsciously when riding a bike, walking or copying down notes.

Reflective thinking would include thinking about the consequences of our actions and deciding on the relative importance of factors affecting our decisions about what to think or do.

If my daughter learns to speak or write fluently but does so thoughtlessly or inconsiderately, then she is likely to upset herself and others. If she memorises lots of facts but doesn't learn how to use them wisely, then her knowledge will be limited in its application. I want her, therefore, to have the opportunity at home and at school to improve, among other things, the proficient, reflective and sociable aspects of her thinking.

Beyond Bloom

I have chosen to use the term 'good thinking' rather than 'higher-order thinking' because the latter is most often associated with Bloom's taxonomy. Not that this is a bad thing in itself, but a number of critics have pointed out that Bloom virtually ignores reasoning, and therefore reasonableness, whereas I would be keen to include it in any recommended rubric. In fact, Matthew Lipman, in the introduction to his teacher's manual for Kio and Gus, states: 'Bloom's Taxonomy of Educational Objectives virtually ignores reasoning skills. In light of this, one must wonder how it achieved the canonical position it has held for the past quarter-century'.[66]

To be fair, Benjamin Bloom actually presented a taxonomy of educational objectives[67] that identified three domains of learning: cognitive, affective and psychomotor, rather than just the one thinking-skills taxonomy that tends to be quoted. Since then, eminent theorists such as Lipman, Sharp, Perkins and Costa have also emphasised the affective domain of thinking and the various persistent attitudes, such as curiosity and respect for others, that they refer to as 'dispositions'.

However, it is important to be sensitive to context. It is all very well having the ability (skills) and inclination (disposition) to think well but what if the context demands that we don't apply our thinking in the way that we would feel inclined? For example, being able to spot a flaw in someone's argument and being willing to challenge assumptions may well be applauded under normal circumstances, but what if it were offensive to do so in a particular context? Or to put it another way, reasonableness is not pure rationality; it is rationality tempered by judgement. So this chapter will focus on 'good thinking' that is flexible, insightful and productive, and attempt to present a new taxonomy for good thinking.

Thinking and education

> If we don't become better people from the education that we gain, then what real purpose does education serve? If it is only to 'earn' a living then, are we really 'living'?
>
> (Anon)

Here are just a few of the reasons why I believe that the teaching of thinking should be emphasised in schools:

1 Thinking is needed for a healthy society

All too often individuals, families, organisations and communities live with the consequences of poorly thought-out decisions, biased judgements, unreasonable behaviour, narrow or limited perspectives and unexamined values. Yet if young people (and indeed adults) learnt to be more thoughtful, by asking better questions, articulating problems, engaging in respectful dialogue with each other and thinking collaboratively, then many of these problems could be avoided. Prejudice, or pre-judging, would reduce; knee-jerk reactions would diminish and thoughtless actions would be restricted.

Of course, some of those in power might prefer citizens not to think or, at least, to be obedient, but authoritarianism has often led to war, aggression and inequality.

I do not wish to suggest that an unreflective life is necessarily a bad thing – many unquestioned traditions bring joy to people's lives, and many actions are enjoyable precisely because they appear to be spontaneous. But perhaps we only know these enjoyable actions are harmless because we've thought about them at some point in our lives.

2 Learning 'how' to learn is the key to lifelong learning

A key aspect of schooling, as I have already suggested, is learning how to learn. Perhaps it is even the most important one since without this ability children can never become independent or adaptable learners. As Einstein put it:

The development of general ability for independent thinking and judgement should always be placed foremost, not the acquisition of special knowledge. If a person masters the fundamentals of his subject and has learned to think and work independently, he will surely find his way and besides will better be able to adapt himself to progress and changes than the person whose training principally consists in the acquiring of detailed knowledge.

(Albert Einstein, *Out of My Later Years*, 1950)

Learning how to learn requires that children ask questions, give reasons, organise information, and understand concepts, all of which are skills of thinking. They also need to be able to generalise, find exceptions, challenge assumptions, paraphrase and predict. And since our world is changing more rapidly than at any time in history, it seems that abilities to learn, adapt and use judgement will be of the utmost importance.

3 Thinking enhances the coding and decoding needed for reading and writing

As will be explored later under the section, 'Against teaching thinking', a common argument for not teaching thinking in school is that there are more important things to teach, such as literacy and numeracy. However, as Galina Dolya points out in her excellent book, *Vygotsky in Action in the Early Years*,[68] the best way to help young children prepare for school is not to push them into learning their letters and numbers; instead, she argues, it is better to help them learn how to code and decode a wide range of child-friendly symbols such as pictures, maps, plans and models so that they are 'ready and have the ability to learn' by the time they get to school.

4 Thinking will be tested in exams

It seems very strange that one of the most frequently used arguments against teaching thinking in schools is that there just isn't enough time, particularly given the content-laden curriculum and excessive pressure for pupils to perform well in exams. And yet, take a look at many exam questions: the first few will require straightforward factual answers but attract only a mark or two, whereas the later ones will require pupils to use thinking skills such as reasoning, explaining, comparing and contrasting, and will attract far more marks.

For example, take a look at this question from OCR's GCSE History (Modern World) Paper 1, sat by many 16-year-olds in June 2008, and consider the thinking skills that are needed to answer this question fully.[69]

Even with extensive knowledge of the Depression, how would pupils answer this question fully, bearing in mind it is worth 7 marks (10 per cent of the whole paper), unless they have been taught how to reason, and understand the arguments and counterarguments necessary for 'proving' a case one way or another?

> **7 (b) Study Source D**
>
> Does this photograph prove that Hoover's policies did little to help people during the Depression? Use the source and your knowledge to explain your answer. [7]

Selected questions from national tests in the UK

NB The main thinking skills being tested have been emboldened.

Key Stage 2 SATS – English Test, 2007 [4 marks]
Imagine you are in Class 6L at Fairborne School. Your task is to write a leaflet **persuading** people to look after the environment. The content will include some of the following topics: recycling; litter; wildlife, water use and transport.

Key Stage 2 SATS – Maths Test, 2008 [3 marks]
Jamie draws a triangle. He says, 'Two of the three angles in my triangle are obtuse'. **Explain why** Jamie cannot be correct.

Key Stage 2 SATS – Science Test, 2007 [2 marks]
Jamal says, 'I think if you put the ice cubes inside lots of plastic bags they will stay frozen for longer'. What sort of statement has Jamal made: **an observation, a prediction, a conclusion or a measurement**?

Key Stage 3 SATS – English Test, 2008 [27 marks]
It is better to be underrated by people than to be overrated by them.

What are your thoughts on the statement above? Do you agree or disagree with the writer's assertion? Compose an essay in which you express your views on this topic. Your essay may **support, refute or qualify** the view expressed in the statement. What you write, however, must be relevant to the topic under discussion. Additionally, you must support your viewpoint, indicating your **reasoning and providing examples** based on your studies and/or experience.

GCSE Design and Technology [4 marks]
Study the BBQ fork shown in Figure 5. Give two **reasons** why the fork should not be used without a handle. **Explain** each of your answers.

GCSE English [27 marks]
Choose an event from your past that has special significance for you. **Describe** what happened and **explain** how you feel about it.

GCSE History [6 marks]
Study the cartoon above, published in July 1948, commenting on the Berlin Blockade. **What is the message** of this cartoon? Use details of the cartoon and your knowledge to **explain** your answer.

GCSE Music [12 marks]
This track is called *The Story Continues* from the film *Harry Potter and the Goblet of Fire*. **Identify** six musical features. For each feature, **suggest** a different mood or action it might be describing in the film.

GCSE Physical Education [4 marks]
London has been successful in being chosen as the venue to host the 2012 Olympic Games. (i) **Explain**, using an example, how this could **prove** to be an advantage to London. (ii) Explain, using an example, how this could prove to be a disadvantage to London.

AS Level Geography [8 marks]
With specific reference to evidence from Figure 7, **outline the factors likely** to affect the size and shape of the sphere of influence of Saffron Walden in the area shown on the map.

AS Level Physics [6 marks]
Describe three observations that can be made, and **explain** them using the principle of superposition. You may find it useful to draw diagrams to help in your description.

Analyse	Describe	Group	Respond
Anticipate	Determine	Hypothesise	Sequence
Apply	Discuss	Identify	Simplify
Causal-link	Elaborate	Infer	Show how
Choose	Estimate	Interpret	Solve
Classify	Evaluate	Organise	Sort
Compare	Exemplify	Paraphrase	Summarise
Connect	Explore	Predict	Support
Contrast	Generalise	Question	Test
Decide	Give examples	Rank	Verify
Define	Give reasons	Represent	Visualise

FIGURE 5.1 A sample of the many thinking skills tested in exams

Types of thinking to teach

To some experts, the teaching of good thinking should be concerned with developing dispositions so people become, for example, more curious, strategic, open-minded and evaluative. Other experts focus on skills such as locating relevant information, comparing, synthesising and understanding. Benjamin Bloom emphasises 'higher-order thinking', whereas Matthew Lipman promotes critical, creative and caring thinking.

Having studied many of these approaches, it seems to me that what all good thinking has in common is that it is:

Flexible, insightful and productive

There is limited use for productive thinking if it is not flexible, nor for insights if they are unproductive. Thus, good thinking is a combination of all three of these characteristics.

As an aide-mémoire for planning my lessons and to ensure my pupils developed a breadth as well as depth in their thinking, I developed a taxonomy using the acronym, EDUCERE (from the Latin 'to lead out'). It is, of course, the source of the English word 'education'.

E

Engage

Paying attention, and thinking collaboratively with:
- Verbal acts such as saying asserting, proposing, hinting, inferring, alleging and contending
- Mental acts such as focusing, committing energy and enthusiasm,
  and maintaining concentration
- Physical acts involving positive and interested body language.

For further ideas, see Application chapter, pages 31–44

D

Desire

Having the inclination and desire to:
- Wonder and inquire
- Reflect upon and evaluate ideas and performances
- Take responsibility as well as calculated risks
- Work collaboratively as well as independently
- Imagine new possibilities and be open-minded
- Be resilient and tenacious
- Manage emotions and impulses
- Be thoughtful.

For further ideas, see Application chapter beginning on page 30

U

Understand

Understanding information by:
- Locating relevant data
- Seeking clarity and precision
- Comparing and contrasting
- Sorting and classifying
- Sequencing
- Making connections
- Representing information
- Seeking deeper understandings
- Identifying misconceptions.

For further ideas, see Challenge chapter, beginning on page 51

C

Create

Create new ideas by:
- Looking for alternatives and possibilities
- Generating hypotheses
- Innovating
- Assembling and formulating
- Suspending logic temporarily
- Searching for value
- Thinking flexibly
- Asking 'What if?'

For further ideas, see the work of Edward de Bono www.edwdebono.com

E

Enquire

Enquire about the subject matter by:
- Asking relevant questions
- Defining problems
- Predicting outcomes
- Testing conclusions
- Seeking details to give depth
- Interpreting meaning.

For further ideas, see Questioning section, pages 66–68

R

Reason

Developing reasoning by:
- Giving reasons
- Using precise language
- Inferring and deducing
- Applying logic
- Testing assumptions
- Presenting balanced arguments.

For further ideas, see the section on Critical Thinking, pages 90–92

E

Evaluate

Judging the value of something by:
- Developing criteria
- Checking accuracy
- Identifying improvements
- Testing relevance and significance
- Benchmarking
- Comparing with alternatives.

For further ideas, see Feedback chapter, page 12

FIGURE 5.2 EDUCERE thinking

Arguments against teaching thinking

No chapter on thinking ought to be complete without some arguments against teaching thinking, so here are a few:

1 There is no time to teach thinking skills

The teachers I've met in all ten countries I've worked in so far have complained that there isn't time to teach thinking skills because of an overcrowded curriculum and a government obsession with exam results. Personally, I think there just isn't time 'not' to teach thinking skills, particularly bearing in mind the way exams test thinking (see pages 80–83). However, I understand the pressures teachers are under and can sympathise with the argument.

2 Thinking skills will be learned anyway, without the need for separate instruction

A frequent argument I hear is that most adults are able to think pretty well, despite lacking thinking skills instruction when they were at school. Though this is undoubtedly true, it is also the case that any ability – be it running, writing, listening or thinking – can also be improved with further instruction. This of course then raises a question about which abilities should be prioritised. I address this on page 84.

3 Reading and writing need to be mastered before any thinking skills are taught

Perhaps this most common argument against teaching thinking reflects the worry that it is being taught at the expense of the three 'Rs'; that some children are leaving primary school, for example, being able to spot the 'odd one out' or rank food groups (popular, though basic, thinking skills activities) but are unable to recite their times tables, write persuasively or spell correctly. Although I think this may be right – being literate and numerate are almost unquestionably the main purposes of education – perhaps being literate, numerate and thoughtful might be an even better set of essential aims for schooling?

4 Some forms of thinking get in the way

A course in Lateral Thinking I attended in Malta began with the presenter, Dr Edward de Bono, suggesting that the 'Gang of Three' (Aristotle, Socrates and Plato) were responsible for everything that is wrong with 'western' thinking because they had created an over-reliance in our society on logic and reason. I guess he was saying this to be provocative as well as to lead into the first step of creative thinking, that of suspending logic and reasoning, so that people are prepared to entertain 'creative' ideas that seem 'illogical' at first. Perhaps there is a case to be heard against overvaluing the logical aspects of thinking in all contexts.

5 Thinking skills cannot be generalised because they are all context-specific

Although every discipline might, for example, require pupils to compare and contrast, there is a big difference between asking them to compare two goals scored in a sport with comparing two mathematical equations or three scientific processes. Therefore, instead of teaching generalised skills, we should, instead, teach the subjects and let the thinking take care of itself – for each subject consists not only of content but also of traditions of inquiry and types of thinking.

A few more quotes for consideration:

- A good memory is more useful than an inquiring mind:

  'Some people do not become thinkers simply because their memories are too good.' (F. Nietzsche, 1844–1900)

- People can get by quite happily without thinking:

  'Few people think more than two or three times a year; I have made an international reputation for myself by thinking once a week.' (George Bernard Shaw, 1856–1950)

Cognitive conflict

Thinking lessons require thinking teachers and thinking pupils

One major problem with any thinking-skills taxonomy is how frequently teachers and pupils are able to get through lessons without having to think reflectively at

FIGURE 5.3 Creating cognitive conflict

all. As I mentioned in my introduction to this book (see page 1), there are many occasions – either because of low challenge, a set curriculum or a desire for quick answers – when pupils do not need to think in lessons, except for perhaps some low-level information-processing. A proven way to counteract this problem is to create cognitive conflict.

Cognitive conflict involves setting up a conflict of opinions within a person's mind. This conflict, or dissonance, unsettles the thinker and causes them to reflect more deeply on their assumptions.

For example, if primary children are asked if Robin Hood was a 'good man' they are most likely to say 'yes'. This is thought number one: 'Robin Hood was a good man'. However, if they are then asked whether it would be good if someone in the class stole from a supermarket and gave the proceeds to the poor, their usual answer is 'no'. This then prompts the second thought in their minds, 'it is wrong to steal'.

This conflict of opinion between thinking that Robin Hood was a good man, while also believing that stealing is wrong, is the tension that causes the children to think or reflect more.

Figure 5.3 shows another example, this time of a pupil trying to answer the question: 'What is a friend?' Their immediate reaction is to think of a friend as being someone they trust (Idea 1). But then the teacher suggests that many of us trust, for example, people working for the emergency services but don't count them as our friends. This prompts Idea 2 which, when compared with Idea 1, is what creates the cognitive conflict.

Notes about cognitive conflict

The prime reason for setting up cognitive conflict is that it encourages pupils and teachers to think more deeply.

When pupils know, or think they know, the solution to a problem, they are not inclined to think much about it. However, if they experience cognitive conflict, then the tension between ideas induces reflective thinking.

For example, consider the last time you faced a dilemma. What did you do? Did you seek solutions or alternative answers, try to identify the real problem, ask for advice or think about the relative merits of one approach compared with another? Or did you panic and ignore the problem?

Of course, both responses are common; which one you tend towards will be dependent on many factors (see the chapter on Self-esteem, beginning on page 97). It is the same for pupils. But if we can help them through the panic stage when they are faced with a conflict, they should begin to think with more persistence, purpose and energy. This serves two purposes: by thinking more they work harder for their learning and often attain deeper levels of understanding; the more they think, the 'fitter' they get at thinking and so the more they are willing to think hard in the future.

Characteristics of cognitive conflict

1 Pupils need to accept, provisionally, the differing opinions that cause the cognitive conflict. This is crucial because if pupils immediately reject one possibility, then cognitive conflict cannot occur. Being in two minds will create the impulse to think more deeply and clearly.

This is why in the wobbler notes on pages 59 and 65 I mention that challenge isn't about proving pupils wrong; rather, it is about encouraging pupils to go beyond the easy answer or first response.

2 There are many ways to set up cognitive conflict, including:

- using dialogue, probably beginning with a question about the meaning or definition of a concept (see Wobblers, beginning on page 59);

- comparing concepts with other concepts, including the use of synonyms and antonyms (see Concept stretchers, beginning on page 70);

- reflecting on different uses of the concept in varying contexts, particularly contemporary examples;

- using extension questions to stretch the meaning of a concept, its uses and the ways it is understood (see the lesson plans at the back of this book for examples);

- 'colliding' the concept with another one – sometimes chosen randomly. For examples, refer to Edward de Bono's notion of PO, or provocative operations.[70]

'Do you want to take this cognitive conflict outside?'

3 The ultimate aim is for pupils to set up cognitive conflict for themselves. In the example dialogues in this book, you will notice that the teacher is using wobblers to challenge the pupils. However, there should be a progression from the teacher challenging the pupils, to the pupils challenging each other and, eventually, to individual pupils challenging themselves. And it is in this final manifestation of challenge – pupils challenging themselves – that we see the basis for reflective thought.

The moral purpose of cognitive conflict

Another reason for focusing on cognitive conflict is a moral one. Pupils live with cognitive conflict most of their lives and yet often ignore it. Take for example, the following common opinions:

Opinion one

- If I'm bullied, I should tell the teacher.
- It is wrong to steal.
- You should never lie.
- Drugs are illegal.

Conflicting opinion

- My Dad says if I'm bullied, I should hit them back twice as hard.
- Robin Hood was a good man.
- Don't tell the truth if it will hurt someone.
- Cigarettes and alcohol contain drugs.

These examples of cognitive conflict are commonplace, so why don't our pupils think very much about them? It seems to me that the answer lies in our discouragement of thinking.

More often than not we tell our young people not to worry about the other side to the argument, with phrases such as:

- 'I know your Dad says to hit back but you're at school now, so you must tell the teacher.' (Inference: ignore the conflicting opinion)
- 'Robin Hood was different, he was make-believe. It is always wrong to steal.' (Inference: ignore the other side of the argument)
- 'Yes, I know these drugs have been decriminalised but they are still wrong.' (Inference: ignore the fact that the law has now been changed to allow some drug-taking)

These might seem reasonable things to say in most circumstances but the danger is that by asking our young people to ignore counterarguments, we are actually discouraging them from thinking for themselves. For example, what would be the difference between:

- a teacher saying, 'Ignore what you've been told about drugs freeing your mind or being declassified; the facts are that drugs will mess you up mentally and physically';
- a drug dealer saying, 'Ignore what they taught you at school. Drugs are actually good for you; they'll give you experiences you'd never have without being high'.

Since there is very little difference in process between these two – both are saying, 'ignore one side of the argument' – then what is to stop children developing the sort of shallow thinking that leads to the 'I was told to do it' excuse of so many defendants at the Nuremburg trials?

The solution to this problem lies, first, in learning how to deal with cognitive conflict in a reasoning and reasonable manner and, second, in encouraging young people to recognise when there is a potential conflict in their thinking and/or actions.

For example, we might ask younger children to decide whether animals can talk or not (bearing in mind the conflicting messages from experience, stories and science). We might ask older pupils to consider not whether bullying is wrong but what bullying is. For example:

Idea 1: Bullying is about making someone feel bad.

Idea 2: It would make someone feel bad if I told them their cat had died but this wouldn't normally be bullying.

NB There are a number of examples of this in the lesson plans at the back of this book.

A quick guide to critical, creative, caring and collaborative thinking

Thinking takes many forms, from innovative to logical, reflective to impulsive, and independent to collaborative, to name just a few. A short introduction to critical, creative, caring and collaborative thinking follows, because these forms of thinking will enhance, and be enhanced by, the lesson plans in this book.[71]

Critical thinking

The basis for critical thinking is argumentation. To most laymen argumentation has something to do with being argumentative, or engaging in a disagreement, conflict or debate. However, in critical thinking an argument is a statement that is:

- an opinion (or conclusion)
- supported by a reason (or premise)
- intended to be persuasive

Further reading

By far the best guide to critical thinking comes from Dr Roy van den Brink-Budgen, former chief examiner for OCR's AS Level Critical Thinking course. His website www.ifthen.co.uk has links to publications and his new online course.

To begin developing critical thinking, the simplest, yet most effective, start is to encourage pupils to back up everything they say with a reason. If they offer the opinion that 'stealing is wrong', then we should ask them to justify their opinion with a reason, such as: 'because it makes people feel bad' (although their first response is often 'just because', or the circular argument, 'because it's wrong to steal').

For example:

> 'I reckon Manchester United is the best football team in the world'.

This is merely (deluded) opinion.

> **Pupil A:** 'Manchester United is the best football team.'
> **Pupil B:** 'No they're not; Barcelona is.'

This is an exchange of views.

> 'Manchester United is the best team in the world because it has won more Premier League titles than any other team.'

This is an argument because a reason is given to support the opinion.

> 'The shop closes at 5p.m. because that's what it says on the door.'

Although this has the form of an argument (conclusion supported by a reason), it's not an argument because it doesn't intend to persuade.

Once pupils have started to get into the habit of giving reasons, we can then ask them to consider whether the reasons they have given support their conclusions (opinions), as well as how strong the reasons are:

> **Argument:** Cars should be banned because they emit dangerous greenhouse gases.
> **Challenge:** Should everything that emits CO_2 be banned? For example, pets, farm animals, people?

Note that the challenger is not agreeing or disagreeing; instead they are questioning the validity of the reason.

> 'Critical' comes from the Greek word, *kritikos*, meaning 'able to make judgements'.
> Source: Online Etymology Dictionary (www.etymonline.com)

> Full entry: 1583, from L. *criticus*, from Gk. *kritikos* 'able to make judgements' from *krinein* 'to separate, decide'. The English word always had overtones of 'censurer, faultfinder'. Critical in this sense is from 1590; meaning 'of the nature of a crisis' is 1649.

Thus, a good rule of thumb for whether pupils are engaging in critical thinking is to discover whether they are making their own judgements, based on the evidence and arguments available, or whether they are simply offering received opinions.

Creative thinking

Considering that Edward de Bono has written approximately eighty books about creative thinking, there's no way I can do justice in this section to such a broad field. However, here are a few key points and pointers:

Suspend logic

One of the best starting points for creative thinking is to suspend logic and reason, come up with some new ideas and then search for the value in any or all of them.

For example:

Scenario: Think about building a new school with no classrooms in it (this seems illogical and therefore stupid, but to innovate we need to go beyond the typical).

Possibilities: Negotiable spaces, movable walls, pupils create classrooms in new ways each year, outdoor spaces used more, altered curriculum timing to suit the space.

Value: Enhanced use of wireless technologies, increased visibility of teaching and learning, pupils learn to negotiate more, increased motivation to use community facilities such as libraries.

Challenge norms

Some effective techniques for encouraging original thought, or lateral thinking as de Bono calls it, include:

Random input: Select a word at random (e.g. tree) and apply the qualities of this object to the subject you are considering (e.g. teaching).

Suspend or challenge: Assumptions (e.g. teaching is done by teachers), boundaries (e.g. teaching only takes place in school) or necessities (e.g. teachers are needed in schools).

In this way you begin to explore and, later, assess the possibilities of a context in which these qualities are absent.

Collaborative thinking

Here are some useful short activities with which to develop collaborative thinking and help pupils prepare to become part of a community of inquiry.

Stand up: Sit in a circle. One person stands up, says 'one' and remains standing. The next person stands up, says 'two' and also remains standing. This continues until everyone is standing. The challenge is that the order in which people stand up should be random, and if two or more people attempt to stand up at the same time, then everyone sits down and the game starts again.

Repeat: Ask a handful of pupils to enact an argument (see Critical thinking on page 90) about a particular topic, then have others repeat what they said. This can be done in pairs or in front of the whole class.

Paraphrase: Ask another three or four pupils to enact an argument but this time ask other pupils to paraphrase what has been said. Check back with the first set of pupils for accuracy.

Build: Once the pupils have developed their paraphrasing abilities, ask them to add to the arguments of others by offering additional reasons.

Challenge: Finally, ask pupils to challenge each other's arguments either by testing their conclusions, questioning their reasons or presenting counter-arguments.

Think left and think right and think low and think high.
Oh, the thinks you can think up if only you try!

(Theodor 'Dr Seuss' Geisel, 1904–1991)

Caring thinking

I've found that there is one main obstacle to communication: people's tendency to evaluate. Fortunately, I've also discovered that if people can learn to listen with understanding, they can mitigate their evaluative impulses and greatly improve their communication with others.

(Carl R. Rogers)[72]

Caring thinking concerns itself with thinking about others and trying to understand them better. The following activities can help pupils to 'listen with understanding'.

Clarifying and responding to arguments (pupils work in groups of three)

1 Pupil A describes their thoughts/arguments about a particular topic (3 minutes).

2 Pupils B and C ask clarifying questions (2 minutes).

3 Pupils B and C then discuss what they think Pupil A means, and what they think in response. Pupil A should just listen (3 minutes).

4 Pupil A now responds either by clarifying or offering additional information/ argument (2 minutes).

5 Pupils B and C brainstorm responses to Pupil A's argument, by identifying the strengths of the argument and foreseeing how others might respond if they heard it.

Making interventions in class discussion to help pupils listen with understanding

1 Pupil A gives an argument or opinion.

2 Teacher asks other pupils, 'Does anyone think they know what Pupil A is trying to say?' and then asks anyone who says 'yes' to explain their understanding of the argument.

3 Pupil A is then invited to respond to this, giving additional detail or a different explanation if necessary. The focus is thus on understanding (and caring about) what others have said, rather than on agreeing or disagreeing prematurely.

Top 10 FACTS for thinking

1 There are two main types of thinking: routine and reflective

Routine thinking is what we do almost subconsciously when completing tasks that are easy for us, whereas reflective thinking includes thinking about the consequences of our actions and deciding on the relative importance of factors affecting our decisions about what to think or do.

2 Thinking skills make up just one third of Bloom's taxonomy of educational objectives

Benjamin Bloom[73] recognised the importance of dispositions and psychomotor responses, as well as the higher and lower order thinking skills that tend to be quoted. This suggests, then, that any thinking programme ought to be similarly balanced between skills, attitudes and dispositions.

3 Thinking skills are tested in exams

The first few questions in most exams require straightforward factual answers, whereas the later ones test thinking skills such as reasoning, explaining, comparing and contrasting – and they attract far more marks.

4 Despite this, many pupils are able to complete tasks without needing to think deeply

Even though some pupils are able to succeed in lessons because they have learned to memorise and repeat, there is still a need for challenging learning in order to develop appropriate ASK.

5 Critical thinking comes from the Greek, *kriticos*, meaning 'able to make judgements'

A good way to determine if pupils are engaging in critical thinking is to identify when they are making their own judgements, based on the evidence and arguments available, rather than simply offering received opinions.

6 Argumentation is the basis for critical thinking

In critical thinking, an argument is a statement that: a) is intended to be persuasive, b) has a conclusion and c) is supported by at least one reason. Without all three aspects, a statement is not considered to be an argument; it is probably prejudice or a difference of opinion based on unexplored assumptions.

7 Cognitive conflict provokes pupils to think more

Cognitive conflict is about setting up a conflict of opinions within a pupil's mind. The conflict unsettles and deepens the pupil's thinking and may help them to develop resources (skills and dispositions) for future use.

8 Cognitive conflict develops a pupil's moral compass

We develop reasoned judgement in pupils by encouraging them to think through their own cognitive conflict. This, in turn, helps to develop the habit of moral decision-making as opposed to moral obedience.

9 Creative thinking often relies on the suspension of logic and reason

One of the best ways to stimulate creative thinking is to suspend logic and reason, create new ideas and then evaluate them. This allows far freer and more extensive exploration of new and innovative ideas.

10 Collaborative and caring thinking are necessary features of a balanced thinking curriculum

Independent thinking is a crucial outcome of education but so is inter-dependent thinking, particularly given the social-networking society that exists today. Thus, approaches to developing collaborative and caring thinking, such as the community of inquiry, are key aspects of any thinking curriculum.

6

Self-esteem

FEEDBACK
APPLICATION
CHALLENGE
THINKING
SELF-ESTEEM

'The gem cannot be polished without friction, nor a person perfected without challenges.'

创业板不能抛光没有摩擦，没有一个人没有完善的挑战。

(Chinese proverb)

Self-esteem and self-efficacy

Definitions of self-esteem vary considerably, although a common thread that runs through most definitions is the issue of the ways we appreciate and value ourselves.

Self-esteem can be broken down into:

■ how highly I value myself;

■ how convinced I am of my own skills and abilities;

■ whether I think I am in control of my own life;

■ the extent to which I believe I am able to achieve my goals.

Although 'self-esteem' is sometimes thought of as a modern-day obsession, many experts believe the term was first used by John Milton in 1657. Perhaps the best-known tool for measuring self-esteem comes from the work of Morris Rosenberg who, in the mid-1960s, developed the Rosenberg self-esteem scale.[74]

In the 1970s, Stanford psychologist Albert Bandura described a trait called 'self-efficacy' as 'the unshakable belief some people have that they have what it takes to succeed'. Unlike self-esteem, which is used to describe a feeling of self-worth, self-efficacy is a judgement that a person has specific capabilities that will lead to success. Interestingly, a key part of developing self-efficacy is failure. According to Bandura, 'People need to learn how to manage failure so it's informational and not demoralising'.[75]

> I've missed more than 9,000 shots in my career. I've lost almost 300 games. Twenty-six times I've been trusted to take the game-winning shot and missed. I've failed over and over and over again in my life. And that is why I succeed.
>
> (Michael Jordan, 1963–)

Maslow's hierarchy of needs

An exploration of self-esteem would not be complete without paying attention to Maslow's hierarchy of needs. In his 1943 paper, *A theory of human motivation*, Abraham Maslow proposed a hierarchy of five levels of basic needs, as shown in Figure 6.1.

Maslow believed that a person would not feel the second need (safety) until the demands of the first need (physiological) had been satisfied, nor the third, until the second had been satisfied, and so on.

Within the esteem level, he noted two versions: a lower one and a higher one. The lower one is the need for the respect of others, the need for status, recognition, fame, prestige and attention. The higher one is the need for self-esteem, strength, competence, mastery, self-confidence, independence and freedom. Beyond these levels, a person needs such qualities as understanding, aesthetic appreciation and spiritual needs.

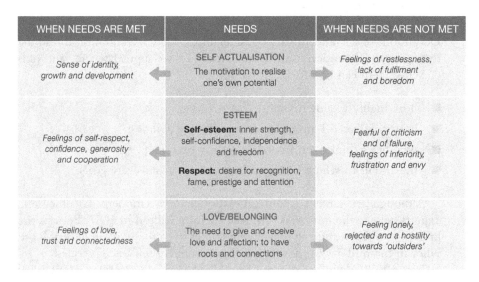

WHEN NEEDS ARE MET	NEEDS	WHEN NEEDS ARE NOT MET
Sense of identity, growth and development	**SELF ACTUALISATION** The motivation to realise one's own potential	*Feelings of restlessness, lack of fulfilment and boredom*
Feelings of self-respect, confidence, generosity and cooperation	**ESTEEM** **Self-esteem:** inner strength, self-confidence, independence and freedom **Respect:** desire for recognition, fame, prestige and attention	*Fearful of criticism and of failure, feelings of inferiority, frustration and envy*
Feelings of love, trust and connectedness	**LOVE/BELONGING** The need to give and receive love and affection; to have roots and connections	*Feeling lonely, rejected and a hostility towards 'outsiders'*

FIGURE 6.1 Maslow's hierarchy of needs[76]

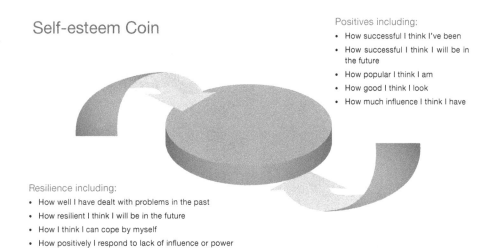

Self-esteem Coin

Positives including:
- How successful I think I've been
- How successful I think I will be in the future
- How popular I think I am
- How good I think I look
- How much influence I think I have

Resilience including:
- How well I have dealt with problems in the past
- How resilient I think I will be in the future
- How I think I can cope by myself
- How positively I respond to lack of influence or power

FIGURE 6.2 Visualising self-esteem as a two-sided coin

Whether Maslow's model reflects real life is open to debate, particularly given the sense that many of the world's most spiritual individuals are also among the poorest people, with the lowest physiological and safety levels. Nonetheless, it is a useful model in that it rightly places self-esteem within a context of other human needs.

Two sides to self-esteem

In my opinion, self-esteem is a balance between success and failure; it is a combination of how successful a person thinks they have been/will be, together with how they think they have coped/will cope with setbacks and failure. In this sense, it is rather like a two-sided coin as shown in Figure 6.2.

If it is true that self-esteem is something akin to a two-sided coin, then there are implications for how we praise pupils. If we only ever help them to succeed, and praise them for doing so, then they will struggle to develop the resilience side of their coin. Similarly, if children only ever experience failure and problems, then they will become discouraged.

In her introduction to *Self-theories*, Carol Dweck refers to this when she says:

> You might think that students who were highly skilled would be the ones who relish a challenge and persevere in the face of setbacks. Instead, many of these students are the most worried about failure and the most likely to question their ability and to wilt when they hit obstacles.[77]

That is why the lesson plans and the Learning Pit model in this book are designed to make things more difficult for pupils, not less. They are designed not only to help pupils learn how to succeed but also how to cope with challenges and barriers

to learning, so that in overcoming these hurdles they develop resilience and hardiness, qualities that perhaps they didn't think they had.

For further information about developing self-esteem with the Learning Pit model, please refer to Stage 2 of the model beginning on page 111.

> 'Success is the ability to go from failure to failure without losing your enthusiasm.'
>
> (Winston Churchill, 1874–1965)

Building self-esteem with praise

In September 2000, I co-founded a social regeneration project in Berwick-upon-Tweed, with the aim of improving the educational and social outcomes of children and young people in the area. We named this project RAIS (Raising aspirations in schools), thinking that if we could boost self-esteem and aspirations, then educational outcomes would necessarily improve. We were moderately successful; we grew into a multi-million-pound project and worked with parents and community groups as well as schools. However, our success was probably due more to a sense of collaboration with the project among the teaching community in Berwick, and the use of P4C, than it was to our work on self-esteem.

Though we did have some success with the self-esteem work, it was limited by our naïve belief that praising more and helping children to succeed more would boost self-esteem. We were almost oblivious to the idea that praise doesn't always help and that success isn't always the best way to boost self-esteem – until we read the work of Carol Dweck.

In her books, *Self-theories* and *Mindset*, Carol Dweck, Professor of Psychology at Stanford University, describes how praising pupils for always getting full marks might have a negative impact, because they are more likely to be devastated or, at least, dispirited if and when they encounter failure – which may lead to an avoidance of risk and a preference for the easy option.

A similar problem is often created by parents who over-praise their children. For example, they might tell their child that she is the best runner, or clever for tidying her room, but then when she doesn't win a running race or doesn't tidy her room, she may no longer feel talented or valued. More examples of these sorts of problems are given on page 102.

> It has become a common practice to praise students for their performance on easy tasks, to tell them they are smart when they do something quickly and perfectly. When we do this we are not teaching them to welcome challenge and learn from errors.
>
> We are teaching them that easy success means they are intelligent and, by implication, that errors and effort mean they are not.
>
> What should we do if students have had an easy success and come to us expecting praise? We can apologise for wasting their time and direct them to something more challenging.
>
> In this way, we may begin to teach them that a meaningful success requires effort.
>
> (Dweck, 2000)[78]

To overcome the potential problems of praising too easily, I used to give pre-tests to my pupils. For instance, with the spelling tests I was obliged to give each week, I would give them the list of words on a Friday afternoon, then test them just 5 minutes later. Of course, many pupils complained about this but I would say that the pre-test was designed to help me set suitably challenging homework for everyone so that no one wasted time doing easy work. For example:

Year 5 spellings to learn for next week

thoughtful

understanding

decision

creativity

exclamation

argument

forgetfulness

memorise

belief

wisdom

Using pre-tests to ensure praise is credible

1   Allow all pupils to study the list of words.
2   Just 5 minutes later, give a pre-test.

3   If any pupil gets 7, 8, 9 or 10 out of 10 on this pre-test, apologise for wasting their time and say you'll find them an additional list of words that would be a more suitable challenge for them. (NB If I thought some pupils were purposely spelling words incorrectly so as to avoid the harder list, I would suggest that from now on they should study the words given to younger classes in the school, seeing as they didn't like learning. They always declined this 'offer'!)

4   If any pupil spells 3, 4, 5 or 6 out of 10 words correctly, confirm that is the list of spellings they need to learn for the following week.

5   Ensure that any pupil with less than 3 out of 10 correct gets the coaching they need to learn these and other spellings in future.

Unfortunately, the misuse of praise is pervasive; it seems to be a common feature of family as well as school life. Take a look at these well-used forms of praise and the associated problems with each one:

- 'You're a fantastic swimmer', after a child has swum a short distance by themselves.

  Potential problem: the child stops stretching themselves further, believing they have now mastered the skill.

- Non-specific praise such as 'Well done!' or 'Brilliant!'

  Potential problem: the child doesn't understand what action is being praised. For example, I often ask children what 'good listening' involves, to which I regularly get the answer of fingers on lips and sitting bolt upright!

- When parents have a race with their young children, they always let them win.

  Potential problem: these children may find it difficult to cope with not winning every race once they get to school.

- Parents say, 'Well done, what a clever girl' after their daughter eats everything on her plate.

  Potential problem: finishing a meal might mean a child is polite but does it mean they are intelligent?

- Computer games for young children give over-the-top praise for completing a task even if that task was easy.

  Potential problem: players prefer to stick to the easy levels rather than risk failing at harder ones.

- Teachers praise pupils every time they get 10 out of 10 on a task or test.

  Potential problem: pupils are learning that they are more likely to be praised for getting everything right, even if it's on an easy test, than for having a go but not getting everything right on a more challenging test.

Take this example, common in schools around the world: so-called 'gifted and talented' pupils are given all the praise for being brilliant; so-called 'special needs' children are given extra praise because we feel sorry for them and believe their self-esteem will be boosted by being told they are lovely, wonderful people; and so-called 'average' children are often overlooked because they're 'just doing OK'.

'Gifted' children

- Recognised by teachers and peers for being outstanding.
- Regularly win prizes and make school or class captain, thus attracting envy from peers.
- Tempted to rest on their laurels because they are always going to be the 'best' readers anyway.

'Average' children

- Often overlooked because they are neither brilliant nor struggling.
- Regularly told they are 'just doing OK'.
- Read well but are told they should try to be more like the gifted children.
- Would really like more praise but realise they either have to be brilliant or 'special needs' to get it.

'Special needs' children

- Get lots of encouragement.
- Are told regularly that they are talented (to boost their self-esteem).
- Read poorly but are assured that they are 'good' readers (which undermines any claim that other, more proficient readers are also good readers).

The problem with praise often begins very early. In Figure 6.3 you'll see two pictures drawn by 4½-year-old Ben for his mother, who just happens to be an art teacher. The first picture took Ben 40 minutes of very deliberate and careful drawing to create. It shows him and his dad fishing together along the local Northumberland coastline. When he presented the drawing to his mother, she praised him for the wonderful job he had done and hung it up on the kitchen wall.

Less than 5 minutes later, Ben returned to the kitchen with the second picture and asked his mother to put it up on the wall next to the first one. In some ways, the praise had been great because it encouraged Ben to draw another picture, but notice there was a drop in quality between the first and the second picture.

It seems that, inadvertently, the praise his mother had given him drew his attention away from engaging in the task for the love of drawing and moved it towards completing another drawing quickly for the love of praise.

A similar thing happened some while ago in my household. My daughter, then 2½, was dancing to some music when her grandmother let herself into the house (as she does every day) and promptly applauded Ava for her dancing. Ava obviously

FIGURE 6.3 Pictures by 4½-year-old Ben

enjoyed this praise and so applauded herself too. However, because she had stopped dancing to applaud herself, her grandmother stopped clapping because there was now no performance to applaud. Having enjoyed the praise, my daughter danced for another two or three seconds and then beckoned for her grandmother to applaud again, which she duly did. So grandmother – who, despite her daily breaking and entering habits, dotes on Ava – had quite inadvertently shifted the focus away from the pleasure of the activity to the pleasure of being praised.

Though these events may just be one-offs, there is a danger that a pattern of behaviour develops such that Ben and Ava choose to engage in activities for the extrinsic praise they are likely to receive rather than the intrinsic pleasure they may feel from the activity itself.

In the case of Ben, his mother's initial response was fine: 'Wow, that's a gorgeous picture! I love the straight lines you've used for the boat and how colourful you've made the sun. Let's put this on the wall together.' However, after praising the first drawing, she might suggest to Ben that he tries something a little different next time so that he knows he'll be praised more for stretching his talents than for doing the same thing again.

Then, if Ben were to return with the second picture just 5 minutes later, his mother could have said, without him being too shocked and disappointed by her reduced enthusiasm, 'That's nice, Ben, but I thought you were going to try something a little different. Tell you what, why don't you cut the boat out and stick it onto some card? Then, you could put it into a tray of sand and build a beach scene. I'd love to see you have a go at that'.

To some people, this might seem as if I'm suggesting Ben's mother becomes a 'pushy parent' but that's not my intention. Instead, the idea is to encourage Ben to believe that having a go at new things and stretching himself is preferable to working out what will attract praise and then doing that same thing over and over.

As for Ava and her dancing, the better option, instead of simply applauding, would have been to get up and dance with her, thus showing that it is the enjoyment of dancing that is special, not the praise that her dancing might attract. That said, when we did just that the next time, we found ourselves dancing for more than an hour, so perhaps it might have been better just to stick to the applause!

Please note that these recommendations are not synonymous with the 'two stars and a wish' routine used so often in schools. Unlike this convention, which seeks to identify two things a child has done well and one thing that they need to improve on every piece of work, I think it's better to say that some pieces of work are, in fact, great just as they are. However, when it comes to the next piece of work, the pupil could try something slightly different so that they continue to learn and make progress.

'Nice effort Alex! Now if you could just think about your posture a bit more son; try lifting your head, sticking your chin out and stretching that back of yours.'

If you have flicked through these last few pages, there is a danger you might have got the impression that I think praise is a bad thing. This couldn't be further from the truth. Praise is a very pleasant and necessary part of human interaction. There are, however, some dos and don'ts for praise, including:

Praise should be credible

There is no point in saying that a pupil is a good reader when it's obvious to her, and to her peers, that she isn't when compared with others in her age group. Not only is she likely to reject this as 'pity praise' but it will reduce the credibility of praise for other pupils as well. However, we can and should praise pupils for their effort and the progress they are making.

For example:

'How wonderful to hear the difference in how you're reading now compared to last week, Sumitha.'

NOT 'You're an excellent reader, Sumitha.' (Particularly when Sumitha is 12 and reading a book aimed at 6-year-olds.)

Praise should develop a growth mindset

Building on the theory of fixed and growth mindsets covered on pages 45–48, our praise should aim to build a growth mindset in every child; that is to say, we should aim at praising pupils for their effort, application, tenacity and willingness to face a challenge, as opposed to simply praising them for getting some things right, particularly easy things.

For example:

'Good for you Julie! I'm really impressed that you had a go at the more challenging option and look what you've learnt by doing it. Well done you.'

NOT 'Well done, Julie. You got everything right; I'm proud of you.' (When Julie has chosen the easy option so as to have more chance of success.)

Praise should be specific

Try to give as much detail as possible when praising. For example, praise a particular action rather than the child (in the same way that we should avoid negative labels for children and focus instead on negative actions).

For example:

'Excellent, Sam. Thank you for turning your head, giving me eye contact and paying attention.'

NOT 'Excellent, Sam, thank you.' (The reason is that other pupils might think that what's being praised, and therefore what's important, is Sam putting his finger across his lips, not the fact that he is paying attention).

Praise should focus on actions not ability

This is straightforward enough but, if my personal experience is anything to go by, it is devilishly difficult to praise the actions rather than the abilities of children, for example, saying 'nice running' rather than 'nice runner', or 'good reading' rather than 'good reader'.

For example:

'Wonderful running, Tommy'

NOT 'You really are a great runner, Tommy'.

Praise personal progress rather than compare one pupil with another

In order to lead to positive outcomes, praise should be focused on the progress a pupil has made rather than on his or her performance or abilities in relation to others.

For example:

'What wonderful progress you're making, Sam. Last time I heard you read, your pace was a bit on the slow side but now there really is a nice tempo to your reading.'

NOT 'Well done, Sam. You're almost as good as Muhammad now. Keep it up'.

Top 10 FACTS for self-esteem

1 Self-esteem affects learning

Although it is almost impossible to determine an exact causal link between self-esteem and achievement, it seems apparent that the best learners have high self-esteem, and that the worst have low self-esteem.

2 Self-esteem has a resilience dimension

Pupils' self-esteem is not reliant solely on believing they have been and will be successful; it is also dependent on knowing they can cope with setbacks and failure, and that they are resilient learners/people.

3 Self-esteem and challenge: a chicken or egg scenario

To develop high levels of self-esteem, pupils need to know they can overcome challenges but, often, they are unwilling to tackle challenging circumstances unless they have high levels of self-confidence.

4 Inner strength is a higher form of self-esteem than prestige or fame

According to Maslow's hierarchy of needs, there is a lower form of self-esteem involving recognition by others, status and even fame, whereas a higher form of self-esteem involves inner strength and independent thought.

5 Recognition is often the first step to higher forms of self-esteem

As with all the human needs that Maslow identifies, there is a route upwards from one to another. This suggests, then, that pupils have a need to be recognised and held in high regard by their peers and teachers before being able to build their own inner strength and come to believe in themselves.

6 Praise significantly affects self-esteem

Appropriate praise, as well as feedback, will help pupils realise they are being recognised for their achievements which, in turn, will help them to build the foundations of their own self-esteem.

7 Praise determination, effort and hard work

If we always praise pupils for getting things right, regardless of the levels of challenge, then the message they receive is that we value correct answers far more than a willingness to grow and learn. Instead, praise effort and hard work.

8 Gifted and talented pupils often have fragile self-esteem

You might think that students who were highly skilled would be the ones who relish a challenge and persevere in the face of setbacks. Instead, many of these students are the most worried about failure and the most likely to question their ability and to wilt when they hit obstacles.

(Carol Dweck, 2000)[79]

9 Indirect praise can sometimes be effective

If you want pupils to improve, let them overhear the nice things you say about them to others (Ginott, 2004).[80] In doing so, you reduce the chance of them wondering if your praise is artificial.

10 Self-esteem is grown, not given

I've missed more than 9,000 shots in my career. I've lost almost 300 games. Twenty-six times I've been trusted to take the game-winning shot and missed. I've failed over and over and over again in my life. And that is why I succeed.

(Michael Jordan, 1963–)

The Learning Pit

'I never teach my pupils; I only attempt to provide the conditions in which they can learn.'

(Albert Einstein, 1879–1955, Nobel Prize winner, often regarded as the father of modern physics)

In the early 1990s, I created a 4-step inquiry process (Concept – Challenge – Construct – Consider) to use with the classes I was teaching at the time. Then in 2003, I came across the work of Butler & Edwards who described the process of going through a 'pit' during periods of transformational change. I loved the analogy and, together with my pupils, added the '4C steps' to create what I called 'The Learning Challenge.' This was done with the blessing of Dr John Edwards.

Since then the Learning Challenge has been used in classrooms around the world. A quick look on Twitter and on www.jamesnottingham.co.uk/about/learning-pit will show you some examples. The only thing that hasn't stuck is the name:

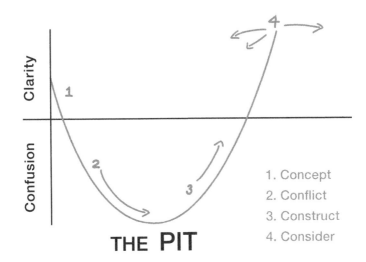

FIGURE 7.1 The Learning Pit

people tend to refer to my model as the Learning Pit even though I call it the Learning Challenge. So, in this edition I call it what everyone refers to it as: The Learning Pit. This chapter will tell you all of what you need to know about it. There is also an animated version of the Learning Pit online at vimeo.com/ 128462566.

The Learning Pit: conditions for success

The Learning Pit is the model I use to explain to pupils why I am challenging them more than they might expect. It is also a pupil-friendly version of the TTM (see pages 53–58). However, before exploring the model in depth, I would like to draw your attention to my underlying assumptions:

1   Pupils are more interested in learning when their teachers are curious and express uncertainty about their knowledge of the world. The Learning Pit therefore assumes a willingness to be perplexed and curious.

2   We are all fallible. The Learning Pit assumes the teacher is willing to admit, or even draw attention to, his or her own errors.

3   Learning is enhanced by participation in guided inquiry.

4   Deep learning comes from understanding relationships between ideas within a subject.

5   Knowledge, understanding, skills and attitudes transcend school subject categories. Therefore, attention should be given to the transferability and connectedness of what is learnt.

6   Everyone who takes part in lessons involving the Learning Pit should aim to be thoughtful, reflective, supportive and reasonable.

7   Though most lessons involving the Learning Pit result in agreement about what answers are 'right', there are occasions, particularly with philosophical questions, when no right answer is achievable. This does not invalidate the experience, since the process of inquiring together, giving reasons and reflecting is at the heart of the Learning Pit.

The four stages of the Learning Pit

Stage 1: Concept

The Learning Pit begins with a concept. The concept can be drawn out from a stimulus such as a story, article or photograph, or is determined directly by the curriculum. So long as most pupils have a basic understanding of the concept, then the Learning Pit can work. Examples of the sorts of concepts that might be suitable can be found on pages 128–134.

'As for teaching children concepts that they have not already acquired in their spontaneous development, it is completely useless.'

(Jean Piaget, 1896–1980, Swiss psychologist whose work focused on stages of cognitive development)

Stage 2: Conflict

As soon as a concept has been agreed, the teacher's responsibility is to create cognitive conflict in the pupils' minds. As described on pages 86–90, cognitive conflict arises when people have at least two opinions in their minds, both of which they agree with, but that conflict with each other. Strategies for creating cognitive conflict can be found on pages 59–64, and there are examples of conflicts below.

Stage 3: Construct

Once pupils have explored their concept for some time (this could be minutes, hours or even days, depending on the concept and on your purpose), some of them will begin to construct a reasonably sound understanding of it. These pupils are then expected to help other pupils construct their own understandings.

Stage 4: Consider

The final stage encourages pupils to reflect on how their thinking has changed, been adapted, assimilated and/or constructed throughout the course of the lesson. Thinking about thinking, or metacognition, is a crucial factor in the learning process. The Learning Pit provides a frame of reference to help structure this metacognitive reflection for pupils.

The Learning Pit in action

Here is an example of the first two stages of the Learning Pit working with 7-year-olds, followed by an example with 14-year-olds. Both dialogues reflect real-life discussions during a couple of recent demonstration lessons I've run. There is an examination of each one afterwards.

The Learning Pit with 7-year-olds:

2, 7 and 8

TEACHER:	Which number is different from the other two and why?
ANDREW:	7, because it's an odd number. (1)
TEACHER:	What's an odd number?
CAROLINE:	A number that can't be divided by 2.
TEACHER:	So, if I have £7, are you saying it can't be divided by 2? How much would each person have if I shared £7 between two people? (2)

CHARLOTTE: £3.50 each.

JAMES: So, 7 can be divided by 2. Does that mean it's even then? (2)

SERGEI: No!

TEACHER: So what is an odd number?

SERGEI: It can't be divided by 2 without leaving a remainder.

TEACHER: But when I divided £7 by 2, that didn't leave a remainder.

DANIEL: But 50p is not a whole number. You can't divide an odd number by 2 without splitting a whole number.

TEACHER: Are you telling me that 50 is not a whole number? (2)

SUNITA: Fifty pence isn't.

TEACHER: This (holding a 50p piece) is not whole? Why not? It looks whole to me.

SUNITA: But it's not a whole pound. It's half of a pound.

TEACHER: So, what is an odd number then?

BEN: It's a number that can't be divided by 2 without changing the units. (E)

TEACHER: Can you give me an example?

BEN: If I had seven pound coins then I'd have to split one of them in half first.

TEACHER: Does that mean anything I have to split in half, so that I can share it, is odd?

BEN: Yes.

TEACHER: But what if I have a £10 note? I would have to split that to share it wouldn't I? Does that make £10 odd?

BEN: Um. . .

Key to notation

(1) – concept is identified

(2) – challenge begins

(E) – eureka moment (see page 118)

The Learning Pit with 14-year-olds:

TEACHER: What is courage? (1)

JONNY: Being brave.

TEACHER: Okay, so what does 'being brave' mean?

SARAH: Facing your fears.

TEACHER: But if I'm scared to run across a motorway, but still do it, am I being brave? (2)

ELLIE: No, that's just stupid. You have to do something good to be brave.

TEACHER: Such as kill someone?

KYLE: That's not good.

TEACHER: But lots of soldiers have been awarded medals for bravery and presumably many of them killed the enemy while 'being brave'. (2)

KYLE: Yes, but that was their job.

TEACHER: So, if I do my job, am I being brave? I'm doing my job now – does that mean I'm being brave? (2)

VIJAY: No, sir. You're not doing your job. You're just trying to confuse us.

(It was very tempting to ask why Vijay thought trying to confuse (or challenge) him wasn't the job of a teacher, but I wanted to stick to the topic).

TEACHER: So, if you're just doing your job then you're not being brave; is that right?
SUNITA: What about firemen? They're brave.
MOLLY: My dad's a fireman and all he does is sit around playing computer games.
TEACHER: But presumably your dad also rescues people and puts out fires when he's asked to.
MOLLY: Of course!
TEACHER: So is he brave then?
MOLLY: Yeh, I guess.
TEACHER: Can anyone else tell me what it is about Molly's dad's job that means he has to be brave to do it?
BEN: He puts the lives of others before himself.
TEACHER: Okay, but most mothers seem to put the lives of their kids, or at least the pleasure of their kids, before their own. Does that mean they're brave? (2)
RACHEL: No, they're stupid. Why give up everything for your kids?
TEACHER: There's that word again: 'stupid'. It sounds to me as if being brave is about being stupid. Is that right?
PUPILS: Not really.
TEACHER: So what does it mean then?
PUPILS: Why don't you tell us?

See page 113 for an explanation of these dialogues.

Key to notation

(1) – concept is identified

(2) – challenge begins

(E) – eureka moment (see page 118)

> 'I cannot teach anybody anything.
> I can only make them think.'
>
> (Socrates, Greek philosopher, 469–399 BC)

The dialogues explained

The dialogues on 'odd numbers' and 'courage' reflect real-life discussions with pupils during demonstration lessons. In both cases, the first thing we did was identify a key concept – marked with a (1) in each case. In the first dialogue, they chose 'odd numbers'; in the second one, I chose 'courage'. Perhaps, in a perfect world, pupils would choose every concept but, with a curriculum to teach, a balance between pupil choice and teacher choice is to be expected.

Once the concept had been identified, I then tried to 'stretch' the concept by attempting to set up cognitive conflict, marked with a (2) in each case. To do this, I used the wobblers described on pages 59–64.

Please note that, as with all the wobblers, my purpose is not to score points or to prove the pupils wrong – far from it. Instead, I try to challenge their first, easy answers so that they need to think again, to reflect more and to try harder. In my introduction to this book, I talk about moving away from the 'Natalie the Navigator' approach to teaching (page 1).

Sticking with that analogy, what I am doing here is putting obstacles in my pupils' way, blocking their normal route so that they have to find an alternative path. I am not saying their normal route is wrong (after all, we usually accept that an odd number can't be divided by two). Instead, it is saying 'this route is OK but for now I'm going to block it so that we can find alternative, and more rigorous, explanations'.

Many teachers ask me why we shouldn't just say 'good answer but can you find another way of explaining it', rather than trying to block pupils' answers. My response is that when a pupil finds one answer (e.g. an odd number is one that cannot be divided by two) they are rarely inclined to search for another, more comprehensive one. Rather, they believe that 'if it ain't broke, don't fix it'. So, in a sense, this blocking approach is temporarily 'breaking' the answer so that pupils feel more of a need to 'fix' it.

Here is a more in-depth study of the Learning Pit.

Stage 1: concept

The Learning Pit begins with a concept. It can be drawn out of the curriculum. So long as most pupils have a basic understanding of the concept, then the Learning Pit can work. Examples of the sorts of concepts that might be suitable can be found on pages 128–134. The key points about this stage are:

A Familiar concepts

Stage 1 of the Learning Pit begins just above the clarity/confusion line, not below it. Unless pupils have some idea of what the concept means then it is going to be very difficult, maybe impossible, to set up cognitive conflict in Stage 2. For example, there would be no point in trying to set up cognitive conflict about 'centrifugal force' with young children because they will have no idea of the concept, let alone two conflicting ideas about it.

That said, there are a number of concepts that pupils do understand to a degree that is not recognised by their teachers. This is particularly the case if we take a concept back to basics.

For example, many pupils in primary schools seem not to know how to use a 30cm ruler correctly, but if we identify the problem as them not always starting at zero then the underlying concept becomes 'always starting at the same point' or 'a fair test'. This concept can then be understood by pupils as young as 5, since they would all believe that, for example, a running race is only fair if all the competitors begin at the same place. This then provides an opportunity to challenge their notions of fairness until they are positively screaming that every test, race or measurement has to start at the same place otherwise it is not 'fair'. At this point, which would be Stage 3 or 4 of the Learning Pit, we can teach pupils that this fair starting point in measurement is referred to as 'zero'. After that, they begin measuring from zero every time.

B Different ways to identify concepts

i) Drawing out

Experienced teachers know the key concepts of their own subject(s). However, that doesn't necessarily make it easy to choose the right concept for the right occasion, when using the Learning Pit. This is why one of the most productive and positive ways to identify a key concept is through the educere approach (see page 84). Essentially, this means lessons begin with a story, artefact or graphic that directs pupils' thoughts towards particular concepts; for example, the cartoon of a dog dreaming, in the Dreams lesson (see page 127) or a group of numbers, as with the 'odd numbers' (page 113). Included with the lesson plans that follow later in this book, I suggest a range of stimuli that you might use.

ii) Using curriculum-specific concepts

If time is short or you feel the need to focus your pupils' attention on a particular concept, then it may be appropriate to select the concept yourself. I would suggest you still use a stimulus to bring the concept alive, but essentially the concept can be picked by you according to your purpose, scheme of work or learning intention. On pages 128–134 there is an A to Z list of concepts that you may wish to use, together with suggested questions for beginning Stage 2 of the Learning Pit. Further examples are available from www.p4c.com.

iii) Preview the concept

One of the best ways to identify a key concept is through the use of preview, an idea explored on pages 42–44. This approach increases pupils' sense of ownership and gives teachers time to think how best to question and challenge pupils' understanding of the concept.

Stage 2: conflict

The second stage of the Learning Pit is to create cognitive conflict in pupils' minds (see pages 59–75). It is also synonymous with the learning zone in the TTM (see page 53). Main points include:

A Basic understanding first

This is a crucial factor. If pupils do not agree with, or have any notion of, the possible meanings of the concept, then cognitive conflict will simply not arise. This is what I meant in Stage 1, point A, when I noted that the concept needs to be familiar to pupils. There is little point in trying to set up cognitive conflict if pupils cannot get their head around even the basics of the concept. This is also why I mentioned earlier the importance of not trying to prove the pupils' theories wrong. If you do, then there is a danger that no opinion will remain with which others can conflict.

B Conflict of thoughts within each person

Cognitive conflict is concerned with creating a conflict of opinions within each person. So, for example, if primary children are asked if Robin Hood was a 'good man' they are most likely to say 'yes'. This is thought number 1: 'Robin Hood was a good man'. However, if they are then asked whether it would be good if someone in the class stole from a supermarket and gave the proceeds to the poor, their usual answer is 'no'. This then prompts the second thought in their minds, 'it is wrong to steal'.

It is the conflict between these two opinions, both of which they agree with, that causes the cognitive conflict, which in turn demands that they think more carefully and deeply about the issue.

C Many ways to set up cognitive conflict

There are many ways to set up cognitive conflict. The main two techniques described in this book are wobblers and scaffolders (see pages 59–70).

'Make-believe or fantasy' – 'Lie or secret?'

Other techniques include:

- Comparison with other concepts using synonyms and antonyms (see an A to Z of Concepts, beginning on page 128).

- Using extension questions to 'stretch' the meanings, uses and understandings of a particular concept (see the lesson plans at the back of this book for examples).

- By colliding the concept with another, randomly chosen, concept. For examples, refer to Edward de Bono's notion of PO, Provocative Operations.[81]

D Life skills developed at the bottom of the pit

On page 34, I identified some of the most common attitudes that teachers wished their pupils had. These include resilience, determination, focus, risk-taking and a positive mindset. These attitudes are developed when we face challenges, such as those encountered in the pit section of the Learning Pit (see Figure 7.1).

'Things that were hard to bear are sweet to remember.'

(Seneca, Roman philosopher, 1 BC–65 AD)

Furthermore, it is important to note that the Learning Pit is designed to be a collaborative exercise. It is not about individual pupils being left in a pit with no support from others. Indeed, encouraging pupils to help each other when in the Learning Pit pit, or guide each other out of the pit can have a significant impact on the social development, empathy and collaboration of pupils.

Stage 3: construct

While struggling in the pit of the Learning Pit together, pupils begin to create an answer through social construction. That is to say, they construct a working definition, or an understanding, through dialogue. An effective example of this came from the demonstration lesson with 7-year-olds described on pages 111–112. We were investigating odd numbers and getting ourselves deeply into a pit. Then one of the boys, who incidentally has 'dyscalculia', said: 'I've got it; it's like odd socks, isn't it?'

I asked him to explain further: 'My mother reckons that no matter how many socks she puts in the washing machine, she always gets an odd number out.'

'What do you mean?' I asked.

'She takes them out, dries them and lays them out on the kitchen table. Then she takes one, puts it together with another, and folds them. She does this until always at the end, there's one left over. Odd numbers are like that, aren't they?'

It was at this point that three children who had recently arrived from Poland had their 'aha' moment. Up to that point, they had been a little lost with what was going on, mainly because of the speed of conversation.

But when they heard Darren describe his mother's odd socks, they instantly knew what he was talking about. Perhaps the same phenomenon can be seen with Polish socks in the wash.

This anecdote nicely describes some of the key features of Stage 3: 1) pupils help each other to learn; 2) knowledge constructed through social interaction is often far more meaningful than knowledge that is served up on a plate by the teacher; 3) pupils who 'teach' are more likely to remember information in the long term than those who are 'taught'; 4) this sort of challenging dialogue often provokes 'eureka' moments.

Eureka is explained further on page 118 but, put simply, it is to do with pupils finding answers for themselves rather than being 'given' answers. In the dialogue about odd numbers, there are two examples of this: the first, marked with an (E), is when Ben realises that units are a crucial factor in determining odd numbers ('an odd number is one... that can't be divided by two without changing the units'); the second 'eureka' moment is when the boy talks about odd socks.

Key points about Stage 3 of the Learning Pit include:

A Considered judgements are the foundations of critical thinking

As noted on page 92, the concept 'critical' in critical thinking comes from the Greek, *kritikos*, meaning 'able to make judgements'. This is what Stage 3 of the Learning Pit is most concerned with: that the pupils do not simply repeat answers received from others but weigh up the pros and cons of each answer and make a decision for themselves. In fact, this seems to be a useful rule of thumb: If pupils are thinking about the concept and coming to their own conclusions, then the lesson is probably an effective one. However, if they are responding with simple, learnt answers, then the level of cognitive challenge is probably insufficient.

B Social construction is a meaningful and significant way to learn

One of the main strengths of the Learning Pit is that pupils co-construct an understanding of key concepts together. Often referred to as 'constructivism' or 'social construction', this approach to teaching and learning has been written about at length, most notably by Lev Vygotsky and Jerome Bruner (both of whom are referred to and quoted in this book). The main features of the constructivist approach are:

- Learning and development is a social, collaborative activity.
- Social construction is connected to 'real life'.
- Constructivism places more emphasis on the social context of learning when compared with traditional didactic methods of teaching.
- Learning is done by pupils rather than done to them.

Self-reflection about: social construction

For further insight into the impact of social construction, please take time to:

1   reflect on your understanding of the concept: challenge;

2   identify three key characteristics of challenge;

3   ask your colleagues what they believe the essential aspects of challenge to be;

4   together, create a rich description of challenge that can be used to enhance challenge in lessons;

5   finally, reflect on the difference between your original definition of challenge and the one that has been created through social construction with your colleagues.

Self-reflection about eureka (see page 118)

For further insight into eureka moments, please take time to answer these questions:

1   How did it feel the last time you experienced a eureka moment?

2   What difference did it make to your understanding and/or knowledge?

3   In what way did it affect your attitude towards learning?

4   How often do your pupils experience their own eureka moments?

5   What could you do to enhance the quality and quantity of eureka moments for your pupils?

C Teaching someone else is one of the best ways to learn

I'm sure many of us have come across the following statistics on learning retention rates:

Pupils remember:

10 per cent of what they hear

20 per cent of what they read

30 per cent of audio-visual presentations

40 per cent of teacher demonstrations

50 per cent of what they discuss

75 per cent of what they practise

90 per cent of what they teach

> 'If you can't explain it simply, you don't understand it well enough.'
>
> (Albert Einstein, 1875–1955)

Unfortunately, these statistics seem to be bogus. Originally, I came across them on the National Literacy Trust website in the UK, though I had previously encountered similar ones from various sources across the world. However, on closer inspection, I found that the only reputable citation was from the work of Edgar Dale (1954) and his 'cone of experience', yet even he doesn't mention rates of retention; instead, his work is concerned with degrees of abstraction.[82]

That said, my own experience is that pupils do remember more when they've been asked to teach other pupils rather than simply take information in. I guess this is not earth-shattering news but I think it is still worth highlighting. The more opportunities we can create for pupils to explain things to each other, the greater the likelihood they will remember whatever it is they are teaching. Whether this is caused by the enhanced levels of cognition required to synthesise knowledge (see Bloom's taxonomy on page 67) is open to debate.

'To teach is to learn twice.'

(Joseph Joubert, 1754–1824)

When I was a Head of Department in the late 1990s, I tried to create a thinking-skills curriculum for my school. My colleagues found that one of its most effective parts involved tasks requiring pupils to create analogies, metaphors, similes or examples. By asking them to do this, we noticed that pupils were having to think more, process more and evaluate more than they otherwise would have done, thus effecting deeper learning. And once the exam results were back, we found that pupils had retained significantly more detail than previously and their levels of achievement were greater.

I now use the Learning Pit as a frame of reference for the setting-up of opportunities for pupils to teach each other. Once I've explained the model to pupils, I am able to ask, 'Who is still in the pit?' and then pair up a pupil still in the pit with someone who has climbed out. The pupil who is out of the pit is responsible for helping their partner climb out; whereas the pupil in the pit should try to find problems with their partner's explanation (this consolidates learning for both parties). Not only is this a lot of fun but it is also an effective approach for developing collaborative learning in the classroom.

D The 'eureka' moment

When pupils have been struggling for a while, perhaps even wallowing in the pit, some of them see the light and have a 'eureka' moment.

In June 2007, I was giving a keynote speech and mentioned the eureka moment. A woman in the audience jumped up and declared she'd just been married! Baffled, I inquired as to the relevance of such a statement. She then revealed (to the 600 people in the auditorium) that her new husband was Greek so she'd been learning Greek, and that 'eureka' was Greek for 'I found it'. Though bemused by her outburst, I was also very interested in this meaning of eureka. It doesn't mean 'My teacher gave me the answer' or that 'Natalie the Navigator told me how to do it'. It means, 'I found it; I found my own answer to this problem and it feels great'.

'I found it!'

Furthermore, when pupils experience the eureka moment, they want to tell everyone about their experience and then repeat it again and again. Compare this with their usual response of 'nothing!' when parents ask what they have done at school that day. However, the eureka feeling simply does not exist unless pupils have initially struggled. If the answer comes easily to them or they are permitted to get away with the first, easy answer, then they are unlikely to experience eureka moments in school.

E Four ways to socially construct

There are many ways to encourage pupils to construct meaning, either by themselves or (more likely and perhaps preferably) in dialogue and collaboration with others. These include:

Key characteristics

Ludwig Wittgenstein (1889–1951), often regarded as one of the twentieth century's most important philosophers, wrote about the problems of language, particularly when attempting to define a concept. In response to the Socratic technique (described in the chapter on Challenge), Wittgenstein said that just because we struggle to define something doesn't mean to say we don't recognise it when we see it. When applied to the Learning Pit, this approach can help pupils arrive at a satisfactory answer (and thus, come out of the pit).

Let's assume that a group of pupils are struggling to define the concept of courage. Every time one of them thinks of a characteristic of courage, another pupil finds an exception to it. Applying the Wittgenstein approach will help them to resolve the dilemma.

1   Suggest that the pupils think of examples of individuals or groups of people whom we would normally identify as being courageous. For example: firefighters, Nelson Mandela, Florence Nightingale, soldiers, the suffragettes, Grace Darling, someone who stands up to a bully.

2   Give the pupils the opportunity to veto any of the suggestions. The list needs to be a combination of individuals or groups of people whom we would normally accept to be courageous.

3   Identify the common characteristics that are the same in all of the cases. For example: taking personal risk, putting others before themselves, standing up for what they believe, believing that they can change things. From this list, pupils are able to construct a full and thoughtful answer to the question.

Hierarchy

Perhaps a more common way to sort out the myriad of answers pupils come up with during the Learning Pit is to rank them. This can be done in a linear rank, a diamond rank (see Figure 7.2), pyramid rank or any such shape that will prompt pupils to analyse the relative value of each answer.

Relationships

Another way to help pupils climb out of the pit is to encourage them to describe the concept they are analysing in relation to another concept. It is useful even, at times, to compare the concept with another, randomly chosen concept, so as to provide opportunities for unexpected discoveries.
For example:

■   what a friend is in relation to a best friend

■   what courage is in relation to cowardice

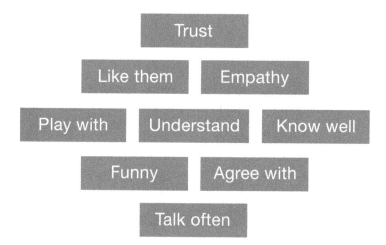

FIGURE 7.2 Using diamond ranking to socially construct the key aspects of friendship

- what real is in relation to make-believe
- what knowledge is in relation to wisdom
- what faith is when compared with belief

For example:

- courage and animals
- understanding and language
- equality and art
- shape and telling lies

Categorise

One technique that is used in a number of examples and lesson plans in this book is that of Venn diagrams. It is a classic way to categorise, and helps pupils to distinguish between two (or more) interrelated concepts.

For example, if the pupils are attempting to define the nature of friendship but get bogged down with the similarities to 'being friendly', then a Venn diagram such as this might help:

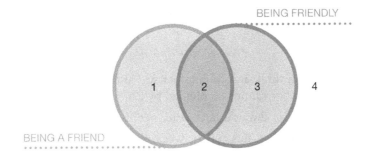

Being a friend – Being friendly

By identifying the characteristics that apply only to area 1, the pupils will be able to more accurately describe the essential characteristics of 'being a friend'.

Stage 4: consider

The fourth and final stage of the Learning Pit is to consider the learning journey. This is where metacognition, or debriefing, takes place.

In his book on *Unified Theories of Cognition*, Allen Newell points out that there are two layers of problem-solving: applying a strategy to the problem at hand, and selecting and monitoring that strategy. Good problem-solving, Newell observed, often depends as much on the selection and monitoring of a strategy as on its execution. The term metacognition (thinking about thinking) is commonly used to refer to selection and monitoring processes, as well as to more general activities of reflecting on and directing one's own thinking.

> Competent or successful learners can explain which strategies they used to solve a problem and why, whilst less competent pupils monitor their own thinking sporadically and ineffectively and offer incomplete explanations.[83]

There is ample evidence that metacognition develops over the school years. For example, older children are better than younger ones at planning for tasks they are asked to do.[84] However, metacognitive skills can also be taught. This final stage of the Learning Pit is designed to help with that.

The metacognitive questions that I recommend are all shaped around the learning (or thinking) journey as described by the Learning Pit. Thus, the first few questions will relate to Stage 1 of the model, the next to Stage 2, and so on. The conclusion of the metacognition stage might also include a reference to the answers that pupils might give if they were asked a connected question in an exam, or involve some reflection on those strategies they used that could be applied to a similar task.

Megacognitive questions for each stage of the Learning Pit

Stage 1

- What did you think an odd number was at the beginning of the lesson? (e.g. 'An odd number cannot be divided by 2')
- What definitions did you hear other people use?
- What were the best bits and/or weaknesses of your first idea?

Stage 2

- What challenged your first idea? (e.g. 'When I realised that odd numbers can be divided by 2')
- How did you feel as you slipped into the pit?
- What strategies did you consider when you were in the pit?
- What were the ideas that you rejected?

Stage 3

- What helped to clarify your thinking?
- Which ideas made most sense to you and why? (e.g. 'The idea that odd numbers can be divided by 2 but we say they can't because when divided they never result in a whole number answer').

Stage 4

- What do you think an odd number is now?
- How do your ideas differ from what you thought previously about odd numbers?
- What strategies did you find useful for dealing with, and then coming out of, the pit?
- What analogy, metaphor or example could you use to explain odd numbers to someone else now? (e.g. 'Odd numbers are like odd socks: there's always one left over. Also, they end in either 1, 3, 5, 7 or 9, and they do not appear as an answer in the 2× table').

The Learning Pit: some final thoughts

The Learning Pit can be a frame of reference

I have shared the Learning Pit with almost every class I've taught. The stages and ideas behind it became a shared language. Phrases such as 'I'm in the pit' or 'I don't understand why some people are in the pit when I'm still at Stage 1' were commonplace. Furthermore, the Learning Pit was a useful metaphor for explaining why I was purposely being difficult and putting obstacles in their way.

The Learning Pit is self-differentiating

'Kites rise against the wind, not with it.'
(Winston Churchill, 1874–1965)

Since lessons that follow the Learning Pit are collaborative, each pupil is able to work at his or her own level. In fact, it is very often the so-called less successful pupils who excel in these lessons whereas the higher achievers, to begin with at least, tend to sit back. There may be many reasons for this, and I am no psychologist, but it seems to me that the lower-achieving pupils are used to struggling, so the pit is familiar territory for them, whereas their higher-achieving peers may fear they don't have the resilience that the pit demands. That said, once the high-flyers realise that the challenge offers a wonderful opportunity to stretch their thinking, they normally involve themselves with enthusiasm (by which time the other pupils have developed more confidence and capacity to 'keep up').

The Learning Pit is a collaborative exercise and helps develop a community of learning

It is important to note that the challenge is designed to be a collaborative exercise. It is not about individual pupils being left in the pit with no support from others. Indeed, the practice of encouraging pupils to help each other when in the pit or to guide each other out of it can help them develop socially.

Encouraging pupils through the Learning Pit increases self-esteem

As has been explored in Chapter 6, self-esteem has a resilience element that is almost impossible to develop without the experience of struggling with and overcoming a challenge. That is what the Learning Pit is all about: creating challenge so that the pupils struggle, but at the same time teaching them ways to prevail.

8

Lesson ideas

'If a doctor, lawyer, or dentist had 40 people in his office at one time, all of whom had different needs, and some of whom didn't want to be there and were causing trouble, and the doctor, lawyer, or dentist, without assistance, had to treat them all with professional excellence for nine months, then he might have some conception of the classroom teacher's job.'

(Donald Quinn, Professor of Mechanical Engineering, University of Akron, Ohio)

Now that all the theory has been covered, here are some lesson plans that pull everything together, beginning with an A to Z of concepts. Each of the ten plans is based on the Learning Pit model.

Pupil materials are available to download in easy-to-photocopy format from www.challenginglearning.com

An A to Z of concepts

Concepts are the foundations of thinking. Matthew Lipman describes concepts as the 'vehicles of thought'[85] and John Hattie remarks that one of the three key factors in pupil achievement is that children be encouraged to 're-conceptualise information' so that they better understand it.[86]

The following is an alphabetical list of concepts that you can use to challenge your pupils to think about in greater depth. They are just a sample of the library of 'concept stretchers' you can find on www.p4c.com

For each concept, start with a 'what is?' question (what is an animal? what is bullying? and so on). When the pupils respond, then challenge them some more, either by questioning their assumptions, testing their conclusions or asking one of the suggested questions below. This works even with very young children (from the age of 4 onwards). Here's an example focusing on the concept of telling lies:

Set up

- Tell an outrageous lie, for example: 'My name is Sam and I'm a hairy gruffalo', but say it with a smile on your face.

- When the children say that's not true, ask the following:

Teacher responses

- How can you tell if someone is telling a lie? (children normally say, 'because they smile when they talk')

- If I smile while I'm talking, am I lying? For example, say something that is very obviously true but with a smile on your face.

■ What about if I frown, does that mean I'm telling the truth? For example, say something that is very obviously false but with a frown on your face.

Further questions:

■ Is it always wrong to tell lies, even if it's to avoid hurting someone's feelings?

■ If I pretend to be a rabbit, am I telling lies?

■ If you tell your mother that you haven't bought her a present when you have, is that lying?

■ Is it lying to say there is a tooth fairy? (for older children only!)

'We learn more by looking for the answer to a question and not finding it than we do from learning the answer itself.'

(Lloyd Alexander, 1924–2007, influential author of fantasy novels for children, including *The Chronicles of Prydain*)

Animal

If I have warm blood in my veins and fur on my back, am I an animal?

What's the difference between an animal and a human?

What is meant by the phrase, 'he was exhibiting animal behaviour'?

What differences are there between zoo, pet, farm and wild animals?

Bullying

If I hit someone, am I a bully? (even if I hit them during a game of football?)

If someone makes me feel bad, are they bullying me? (even if they tell me my cat has died?)

Is it always wrong to bully someone? (what about bullying them into giving to charity?)

Can someone bully you without being a bully?

Creativity

If I have different thoughts and ideas from everyone else, does that make me creative?

Are creative people good at telling lies? Can animals be creative?

Why is it often said that children are more creative than adults?

Different

If two things are not the same, does that necessarily make them different?

Are identical twins different?

If a candle is melted, is the melted wax now a different wax?

Is anything absolutely identical to anything else, or is everything different?

Exist

Does everything that we can think of exist? Do flames exist?

Does the cold exist?

When someone dies, do they cease to exist?

Friends

What are friends?

Do you always have to be nice to your friends?

If a friend won't share their sweets, does that mean they're no longer your friend?

How do you know that someone is your friend?

Ghosts

If lots of people are scared of ghosts, does that make the ghosts real, or are people simply scared of nothing?

The word 'ghost' appears in the dictionary; does that mean ghosts are real?

If ghosts do exist, then are they just people-ghosts or are there animal-, insect-, inanimate object-ghosts?

If everyone in the world believed in ghosts, would that mean they definitely do exist?

Home

Does everything have a home? Do wind and rain have a home?

If a bird's nest is in a tree, does that mean the tree is the bird's home?

What's the difference between a house and a home?

Ideas

Are ideas the same as thoughts?

What does someone mean when they say they 'have no idea'?

What does 'idea' mean in the phrase, 'my idea of good music is different to yours'?

At what age do people have their first idea?

Justice

Is justice always fair?

How are justice and revenge linked?

Is there a difference between natural justice and human justice?

Does everyone deserve justice?

Killing animals

What's the difference between killing an animal and killing a human?

Is it OK to kill some animals but not others? If so, which ones?

Would it be better to kill carnivorous animals rather than herbivorous animals?

If it's OK to kill farmed animals, is it OK to kill pets?

Like

What is the difference between like and love?

What do each of the uses of 'like' mean in the phrase, 'I like lots of things, like chocolate'?

What do each of the uses of 'like' mean in the phrase, 'like mother, like daughter'?

What is the opposite of like?

Mind

Is your mind inside, outside or the same as your brain? Do all your thoughts take place in your mind?

When you talk to yourself, is that you talking or your mind talking?

What does mind mean in 'mind your own business', 'I have a lot on my mind', and 'don't mind me'?

Names

If you had a different name, would you be a different person?

Why do things need names?

How many examples of names for things people do can you think of?

Is 'horse' also the name of a horse?

Original

If I make up a story, does that mean it's original?

When you have an idea for the first time, does that make it original?

Are your memories copies of an original experience?

What's the difference between originals and copies?

Poem

Can a single sentence be a poem?

When can a song be a poem?

Can silence be a poem?

If a poem has never been written down or shared, is it still a poem?

Questions

Why do we ask questions?

What would life be like if you could never ask questions?

Do you ever ask a question, but don't expect an answer? Why/when?

What's one of the best questions you've ever asked?

Real

What does real mean?

Is real the opposite of fake?

Are dreams real?

What's the difference between a real banana and a plastic banana?

Story

Can a story be completely true and factual?

Why is it OK to make up stories but not to tell lies?

If someone makes up a story, does that mean the story can't be real?

If a story includes talking animals, does that mean it's definitely made up?

Thoughts

Do your thoughts control everything you do?

Can two people have exactly the same thoughts?

Are thoughts real or imaginary or something else?

What's the difference between thoughts and ideas?

Understanding

Can a person know something without understanding it?

Can a person comprehend something without understanding it?

Are there things you do without understanding how you manage to do them?

Are you responsible for obeying a rule if you don't understand the rule?

Virtues

Is competitiveness a virtue? Is helpfulness a virtue?

Is the absence of a vice a virtue?

Can a personality trait be both a virtue and a vice (e.g. ambition)?

Worth

How can we tell what a loaf of bread is worth?

How can we tell what a pet is worth?

What is the air worth?

If something is worth a lot, does that mean it's expensive?

Xenophobia

Why are people scared of what they don't know?

Can it be a good thing to be scared of the unknown?

Is it xenophobic to say you are scared of terrorists?

Is it natural to be xenophobic?

You

What makes you 'you'?

Is there only one of you?

When you play make-believe, are you still you?

Would you still be you if you had different parents?

Zoos

Between them, do all the zoos in the world have examples of all the animals in the world?

Why aren't dogs and bunny rabbits kept in zoos?

Is it better for animals to be in a zoo or in a natural habitat?

Should we teach zoo animals things?

Culture

Age range 10–18

Subjects: Humanities, citizenship, media, PSHE, literacy, foreign languages

Stage 1: Identify the concept

The concept of culture is often used in two senses, with two overlapping but different meanings:

- The arts and learning: the special processes of discovery and creative effort.
- A way of life including common meanings, attitudes, values, beliefs, hierarchies, material objects and possessions, modes of perception, and habits of thought and activity.

Teenagers are often keen to talk about their own culture or at least their own developing values, attitudes, tastes and allegiances. They may also feel trapped in a culture or even feel culture-less. They are interested in questions about whether culture is a given or whether it can change; how they are influenced by culture and whether they can influence it; or if they feel influenced by more than one culture, then which are the most important in certain situations?

Indeed, 'culture' is used in so many ways and in so many different contexts, that it is very unlikely you'll be able to develop a complete definition with your pupils. This should not put you off; in fact, it should do the opposite! Often the best (philosophical) dialogues begin with one question and end with many, and the concept of culture will stimulate a lively discussion.

Complexities of the concept:

- How many cultures does one person belong to?
- Can a culture exist with just one person?
- If a person lived as a hermit, would they still belong to a number of cultures?
- Do animals have cultures?

Stage 2: Problematise the concept

The following dialogue with 14-year-old pupils was followed by an activity that required them to list every culture that they belonged to and then identify the characteristics common to each of these cultures.

TEACHER:	What is culture?
SIMON:	A group of people.
TEACHER:	We're a group of people; does that mean we're a culture?
SIMON:	Sort of.
TEACHER:	Do we all belong to the same culture, then?
MOHAMMED:	No, not all of us. Some of us are a different colour, and some of us believe different things.
TEACHER:	Does that mean everyone who's black belongs to one culture and everyone who's white belongs to another culture?
RACHEL:	No, that's to do with race, not culture.
TEACHER:	What's the difference?
SHAHEENA:	Race is the colour of your skin whereas culture is about what you believe and how you act.
TEACHER:	So if culture is to do with what you believe, then if we all believed a particular footballer was the best in the world, would we all belong to the same culture?
TAS:	No, that's just about football.
TEACHER:	Is there no such thing as a 'football culture' then?
TAS:	Yes, there is, but that's about liking football.
ANNA:	And wearing sporty clothes and trainers and things.
ALISON:	I wear sporty clothes but I hate football, so I'm not part of a football culture, am I?
TEACHER:	So, going back to the original question (what is culture?), are we saying that culture is a group of people who like the same thing and perhaps wear the same things as well?
VIJAY:	Yea, that's right.
TEACHER:	But people who like the same thing and wear the same things aren't necessarily of the same culture, are they? For example, what about everyone who goes to see Kylie Minogue live? Presumably, they all like the same thing (Kylie) and maybe all wear Kylie tour t-shirts.
ANITA:	OK, that doesn't work but it does if you think about the Goths. They all wear black and like the same music.
ANNA:	No we don't.
ANITA:	So are you saying you're not part of the Goth culture?
ANNA:	No, I'm not saying that because I am part of the Goth culture but I'm also part of the youth culture and maybe even this school culture, aren't I? But just because you're from the same culture doesn't mean you like the same thing, do the same thing or even wear the same thing.
TEACHER:	So, what does culture mean then?

Deepening the Learning Pit

What is culture?

- Is culture the same as belief? If not, how do they differ?

- If people know your nationality, do they know your culture?

- Are cultures always changing?

- Do people belong to cultures or do cultures belong to people?

- Could a group of people create a new culture?

- Does culture cause people to believe certain things or behave in certain ways? Are we the effects of our cultures?

- Could there be a country in the world with a mono-culture?

- What does it mean when people say that Britain is more multi-cultural now?

- If your mother was Spanish, your father Chinese and you were born in the UK, which culture would you belong to?

- Do stereotypes of cultures have a basis in reality?

- Is language part of culture or is culture part of language?

What TYPES of culture are there?

- Do animals other than humans have cultures?

- Do fish have cultures?

- Is it possible for an individual to have their own culture?

- Is it possible for a person not to belong to any culture at all?

- If a group of people liked exactly the same things, would they share a culture?

- If a group of people thought the same things were important, would they share a culture?

- How big would a group have to be to be thought of as a culture?

- What cultures do you think you belong to?

- What cultures do other people in this group think they belong to?

- Does this group/class have its own culture?

- Why do cultures exist?

Which of the following creatures do you think have cultures?

baboons

fish

dogs

wolves

dolphins

chimpanzees

mice

cats

jellyfish

butterflies

elephants

ants

rats

spiders

ostriches

bees

bats

penguins

What is the VALUE of culture?

■ Are some cultures better than others? If you think 'yes', how would you know? If you think 'no', why not?

■ Should people always follow the values of their cultures?

■ What if the values of two cultures that influence a person conflict? What values should that person take as most important?

■ Think of some cultures you are influenced by. Do these cultures promote identifiable values?

Exploring culture with examples

Are the following examples in Table 8.1 stereotypes or true reflections (or both)?

TABLE 8.1

WHEN WE HEAR/READ THE WORDS . . .	WE THINK OF . . . (CIRCLE ALL THAT APPLY AND ADD YOUR OWN DESCRIPTORS)					
British culture	reserved	innuendo	lager-louts	music	film	
American culture	brash	glamorous	Loud	sporty	television	hamburgers
French culture	wine	laid-back	Amorous	food	smoking	
Indigenous culture	minority	exploited	proud	integrated	marginalised	tribal
Laddish culture	beer	unladylike	drunk	loud	fun	groups
Norwegian culture	Vikings	Fish	skiing	pine trees	reserved	proud
Swiss culture	neutral	Cuckoo	cheese	watches	Geneva Convention	
Aussie culture	barbies	Neighbours	g'day	Bondi Beach	relaxed	
Latin culture	salsa	passionate	olive skin	heat	sexy	tactile
Greek culture	architecture	Adonis	fiery	music	feta cheese	classical
Youth culture	rebellious	energetic	passionate	unruly	gangs	ASBOs
Japanese culture	sushi	reserved	efficient	kimono	karate	tourist
This school's culture						
This group's culture						

Stage 3: Construct understanding

Comparing the concept of culture with other concepts may help pupils to decide whether culture creates traditions, religions, cuisine and so on, or vice versa.

A comparison between 'culture' and 'language' is interesting in that language enables the members of a culture to express and develop shared meanings. It is also a connection between people that has formed the basis of nationalist demands for separateness.

A comparison between 'culture' and 'gang' could lead to a discussion of subcultures and conflicting cultural influences on a person.

A comparison between 'culture' and 'race' raises questions about how the term race is used. Is it used as a synonym for foreigners or for skin colour or facial appearance? Is it used to suggest differences between people that are beyond culture and in this way to justify an ideology of separateness?

What are the similarities and differences between the following pairs of concepts?

culture and family

culture and community

culture and civilisation

culture and gang

culture and language

culture and religion

culture and race

culture and traditions

culture and nationality

culture and environment

culture and nature

culture and cuisine

culture and expectations

culture and education

culture and being cultured

culture and stories groups tell about themselves

Stage 4: Reviewing the learning journey

Possible metacognition questions:

- What cultures do you think you belong to?
- Is it possible for an individual to have their own culture?
- Do people belong to cultures or do cultures belong to people?

- Are some cultures better than others?
- Is culture the same as belief? If not, how do they differ?
- How does your idea of culture differ from at the beginning of the lesson?
- What questions about culture are you left with?

Dreams

Age range 4 years +

Subjects: Early years, science, citizenship, PSHE, literature, the arts, media

Stage 1: Identify the concept

Philosophers are particularly interested in the topic of dreams because of the opportunity that it offers to inquire into other concepts such as thinking, personal identity, the mind, reality and perhaps even time.

One problem you might encounter, however, is that pupils (particularly young ones) will often wish to recount the contents of their dreams. This is not necessarily a bad thing but a lesson or inquiry can lose its focus if too many anecdotes are shared. Try using some of the suggested questions below to help maintain momentum and focus.

If your learning aim is to improve pupils' creative writing, inviting them to share their dreams may be appropriate. As ever, context is really important.

Stage 2: Problematise the concept

Questions to ask young children (3–7) about dreams:

- What is a dream?
- Is dreaming the same as thinking?
- Do you have to close your eyes to dream?
- Do you have to be asleep to dream?
- Do you dream in pictures? Are they in colour or in black and white?
- Are you always in your own dreams?
- Is it good to dream?
- Does everyone dream?
- Do animals dream?
- Can you daydream at night?

Additional questions for juniors (7–11):

■ Are dreams stories?

■ Do dreams have a beginning, middle and end?

■ Do dreams ever come true?

■ Do you have different dreams now to the ones you had when you were a baby?

■ Do you think unborn babies dream?

■ What's the difference between a dream and a nightmare?

■ What's the difference between a dream and a daydream?

■ Can you make yourself dream?

■ Can you control or alter your dreams as you please?

Additional questions for adolescents (11–14):

■ Can you dream and eat at the same time?

■ Can you ever learn something from a dream and, if so, what?

■ Is your sense of space the same in a dream as it is when you're awake?

■ What about time? Is this the same in a dream as when you're awake?

■ Do dreams reflect the past or predict the future, or both?

■ Does the kind of dream you have depend on how you're feeling when you go to bed?

■ Are you the same person in your dreams as you are when you're awake?

■ If you're different, then who is the person in your dreams if not you?

■ Are dreams a reflection of reality or are they entirely fictitious?

Further questions to ask older pupils (14–18):

■ Is there a difference between thinking while you're asleep and dreaming?

■ What are dreams for?

■ Is dreaming purely a human ability? Can animals dream? Could computers ever dream?

■ How is it possible to be dreaming and thinking about that dream at the same time?

■ People often use aspirations, dreams and wishes interchangeably. Are they the same? If not, what are the main differences?

■ What do you think Lewis Carroll (the author of *Alice in Wonderland*) meant when he entitled a poem, 'Life is but a dream'?

■ The philosopher, Descartes (1596–1650), was convinced that there are no definite signs to help us determine for certain whether we are dreaming or awake. Was he right?

- Another philosopher, Immanuel Kant (1724–1804), wrote that 'the lunatic is a wakeful dreamer'. What do you think he meant by this?
- What did William Shakespeare (1564–1616) mean in *Hamlet* (Act III, Scene 1) when he wrote: 'To sleep, perchance to dream – ay, there's the rub; For in that sleep of death what dreams may come, when we have shuffled off this mortal coil?'

Stage 3: Construct understanding

Comparing dreams with other concepts

Venn diagrams for primary school children (5–11):
Add characteristics of dreams and daydreams to a dream hoop and/or a daydream hoop. Then look for labels to go into a Venn diagram on 'dreams' and 'thoughts'.

Additional comparisons for older pupils (11–18):
Pick five of these concept pairs. Describe the similarities and differences between the two concepts in each case.

dreams and reality

my dreams and your dreams

dreams and daydreams

dreams and aspirations

dreams and beliefs

dreams and goals

thoughts and dreams

ideas and dreams

dreams and premonitions

desires and dreams

dreaming and being drunk

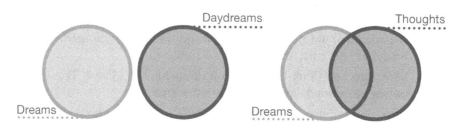

Dreams Daydreams Dreams Thoughts

dreams and fiction

dreams and perception

dreaming and wondering

dreams and visions

dreams and hallucinations

dreaming and imagining

dreams and wishes

dreaming and letting your mind wander

dreaming and making up stories

The 'you' of your dreams and the 'you' when you're awake

Understanding contemporary uses of the term 'dreams'

Explain what 'dream' means in the following examples:

1   Martin Luther King's speech in 1963 that included the words: 'I have a dream that my four little children will one day live in a nation where they will not be judged by the colour of their skin but by the content of their character'.

JNP

2　She was in a dream-like state.

3　He always did dream big.

4　She's so dreamy.

5　He's such a dreamer.

6　My dream car is a Porsche.

7　The politicians are living in a dream world if they think we're going to agree to that.

8　It was a dream move for us.

9　Dream on, mate!

10　Love's young dream.

11　It works like a dream.

12　Dream machine.

13　Dream catcher.

Stage 4: Reviewing the learning journey

Possible metacognition questions:

- How many different uses of the word 'dream' have we thought of?
- In what ways does dreaming differ from thinking?
- Do you always know when you're dreaming?
- In what ways are dreams and reality linked?
- Can you change or affect your dreams?
- Why do you think most of us so rarely remember our dreams?
- How does your idea of dreaming differ from at the beginning of the lesson?
- What questions about dreams are you left with?

Fairness

Age range 4 years +

Subjects: PSHE/personal development, citizenship, humanities/social studies, health and PE

Stage 1: Identify the concept

Fairness is an essential concept for moral and political thinking. That said, learners – particularly younger ones – will probably find it easier to say what is unfair than what is fair. I find that conversations about fairness usually start with the idea that equality is a pretty good synonym for fairness. But that is hard to sustain when scrutinised. What then is fairness? Conversations about fairness in relation to competitive games may raise questions about what people deserve for their talents or efforts.

Potential for challenge

■ Would it be fair for everyone to be treated in the same way?

■ Is there a (moral) obligation for us to be fair?

■ Is it possible or even desirable to be fair?

Stage 2: Problematise the concept

The following dialogue is used to illustrate how we might begin to challenge pupils' understanding of fairness:

Introduction: give a sweet to just five pupils, leaving the others empty-handed.

CHILDREN:	That's not fair!
TEACHER:	Why not?
CHILDREN:	Because we didn't all get sweeties.
TEACHER:	Why should I give sweets to everyone?
CHILDREN:	It's not fair if you don't.
TEACHER:	But they're my sweets so surely I can give them to whom I like?
PATRICK:	But why did you pick those five?
TEACHER:	They're my favourite pupils; what's wrong with that?
CATHERINE:	As a teacher you shouldn't have favourites.
TEACHER:	So it's all right for you to have favourites but not me? Why not?
CHILDREN:	Teachers are supposed to make sure everything's fair.
TEACHER:	Does that I mean I should treat all of you in exactly the same way?
CHILDREN:	Yes, of course.
TEACHER:	So should I give everyone an 'A' for effort, no matter how much effort they put into their studies?
CHILDREN:	No, but. . .
TEACHER:	Or what about adults and children; should they all be treated in the same way?
CHILDREN:	Yes.
TEACHER:	So children, even young ones, should be required to work, should they?
CHILDREN:	No.
TEACHER:	But why not? It's only fair!
CHILDREN:	But children shouldn't have to work; that's what their parents are supposed to do.
TEACHER:	Does that mean it would be unfair of me to ask you to help tidy the classroom? Should we expect someone else to tidy up after us?
CHILDREN:	No, but. . .

Deepening the Learning Pit

Activities/questions for young children (3–7):

Pick two children. Give one of them one sweet and the other two sweets, and ask if that's OK. Swap them around, such that the first child now has two sweets and the other one has one. Is that fair? Now take the sweets away from both of them and give them to other children. Ask whether it's fair now. Also ask: 'Is it fair that I should be able to give my sweets to whoever I want to?' And: 'Is it fair to take something away from someone, once it has been given? Why or why not?'

- Does fair mean being the same as someone?
- Or does it mean everyone having the same things?
- How do you know if something's fair or not?
- Why should people try to be fair?
- What is unfair?
- If Lucy pinches Amy, is it fair for Amy to pinch Lucy?

Activities/questions for juniors (7–11):

Ask pupils to help you set up an imaginary running race and change the variables that make up the teams, asking each time whether the race would be fair.
For example, draw attention to:

- Different length legs.
- Newest trainers versus oldest trainers.
- Boys versus girls.
- Oldest versus youngest
- What would be the fairest way to set up the teams? Give reasons.
- Would a draw be the fairest possible result? Give reasons.
- Could handicapping the best runners (e.g., by giving them heavy rucksacks, staggered starts or obstacles) make the race fairer or would that be unfair to the best runners? Give reasons.
- If a runner is unlucky to get knocked over by accident, is that unfair?
- If a team wins the race by cheating, is that unfair? Why?

Additional questions for juniors (7–11 years):

- What does it mean to be fair?
- If you feel something is unfair, does that mean it is unfair?
- Does fairness mean everyone being equal?
- Does fairness mean everyone being treated in the same way?

- Is it fair to have a party and not invite everyone?
- If I've got a bag of sweets, would it be fair to keep them all to myself?
- Is it fair that some people have more money than others?
- If one child was being bullied in our class, would it be fair if I bullied everyone else so that we were all equal?
- If 28 out of 30 children in our class wanted us to get a pet hamster but one child was allergic to furry animals and one was scared of hamsters then what would be the fair thing to do?

Additional questions for adolescents (11–14):

- Would it be fair to share out all the food in the world equally? If so, would it be fair for me to take food from your house and send it to children who have very little food?
- Would it be fair for everyone to earn the same wage?
- Is it fair to have rich people and poor people?
- Is fairness possible within a family?
- Is fairness possible within school?
- Is it fair when bad things happen to good people?
- Is it fair when good things happen to bad people?
- Would it be fair for someone who's desperate to jump to the front of the toilet queue?

Additional questions for older pupils (14–18):

- Is it fair to always go with what the majority want?
- Is it fair to put on school trips that not everyone can afford to go on?
- Is it fair that 18-year-olds have a lower minimum wage than 21-year-olds?
- Would it be fair to torture the torturer, terrorise the terrorist, or murder the murderers?
- Is fairness possible (or even desirable) in society?
- How could fairness be achieved?
- Is 'survival of the fittest' fair?
- Is it possible to construct a fair test in science?

Stage 3: Construct understanding

The exercise in Table 8.2 may help your pupils to piece together a characterisation of fairness:

TABLE 8.2 Are these examples fair or unfair?

	FAIR	UNFAIR	NOT SURE	REASON
1 Everyone in the school is given the same amount of homework.				
2 Doctors are paid more than teachers.				
3 Men are paid more than women for doing the same job.				
4 Everyone is given a prize on Sports Day.				
5 Children in some countries can't afford to go to school.				
6 Some people live in very big houses.				
7 A starving woman steals a loaf of bread to feed her family.				
8 A pupil steals a CD from a shop.				
9 Children are not allowed to drive cars.				
10 Disabled people are allowed to park for free.				
11 Someone breaks the law so is sent to prison.				
12 A granny can't pay her council tax so is sent to prison.				

Stage 4: Reviewing the learning journey

Possible metacognition questions:

- Is fairness the same as being equal?
- When is it right to treat people 'unfairly'?
- Is it fair that some people have more than others?
- Is it fair that people who work are paid more than people who can't work?
- Is fairness possible or even desirable?
- How does your idea of fairness differ from at the beginning of the lesson?
- What questions about fairness are you left with?

Growth and change

Age range 4 years +

Subjects: Personal development, citizenship, humanities/social studies, literacy, science

Stage 1: Identify the concept

Children and young people are often very interested in the ways they change and grow. Yet although it seems that everything is destined to change in some way, everything does not necessarily grow. For example, the weather changes every day but we wouldn't say it was growing. Thus, comparing these two concepts may be a useful way to help learners explore each one.

Furthermore, when people use the concept of growth, they may refer to an increase in size or quantity. On the other hand, they may use the term as a metaphor for personal or social development. And this 'personal growth' may be qualitative or quantitative, considering whether people are becoming better, more experienced or more capable in some ways.

Change is also a complex concept. In some respects, the world we live in doesn't change very much. For example, the earth rotates around the sun every 365¼ days and the position of the equator remains constant. But in other ways the earth is always changing. In geography, we might study the violent changes that form mountain ranges and, in history, look at the significant changes through the ages. In some subjects, we might even look at how humans have looked for ways to force change – attempts to reverse climate change or overthrow governments, for example.

Potential for challenge

■ What's the difference between growth and change?

■ Is there an opposite of growth?

■ Is there anything that doesn't either grow or change with time?

Stage 2: Problematise the concept

The following dialogue is used to illustrate how we might begin to challenge children's understanding of growth and change, with young children (4–9). Key differences to tease out are growth and development, growing and multiplying, growth and progression, time and growth.

TEACHER:	Do all things grow?
CHILDREN:	Yes.
TEACHER:	Plants? (yes) Children? (yes) Adults? (maybe) What about building blocks?
CHILDREN:	No, blocks can't grow.
TEACHER:	But what if I built a tower with some of the bricks? That would be growing, wouldn't it?
CHILDREN:	Yes.
TEACHER:	So, building blocks can grow?

(They're divided at this point. Some think yes, some no and some are not sure).

TEACHER:	What's the difference between this type of growing and the way plants grow?
CHILDREN:	Plants grow by themselves but you're making the bricks grow.
TEACHER:	But I thought we made all of our plants grow by watering and feeding them?
CHILDREN:	But plants grow outside without our help. The bricks wouldn't do that.
TEACHER:	OK, so growth means changing without our help, is that right?
CHILDREN:	Yes.
TEACHER:	But the weather changes without us doing anything, doesn't it? But weather doesn't 'grow'.
CHILDREN:	No.
TEACHER:	So, what's the difference between growing and changing? Can we think of examples of things that change, things that grow and then things that do both?

Deepening the Learning Pit (4–9 years)

See Table 8.3.

TABLE 8.3

	GROWTH	CHANGE	BOTH	NEITHER	REASON
You get one year older.					
You put on weight.					
You have a haircut.					
You make a new friend.					
A plant gets bigger.					
Your toy gets broken.					
You move to a new school.					
A goldfish dies.					
You learn to play the piano.					
You forget some facts you once knew.					
You learn how to share.					
You learn to be more patient.					
You remember a dream.					
It stops raining.					
You get a new baby brother.					
You build a sandcastle.					

Deepening the Learning Pit (9–14 years)

TEACHER:	What's the difference between growth and change?
MICHAEL:	There's no difference.
TEACHER:	Are you sure? We could say that the weather changes but it doesn't grow, does it?
AMY:	Hurricanes grow in force and intensity.
TEACHER:	Aha, very good. So they are one and the same thing then? Well, let's test that: can anyone think of something that changes but doesn't grow?
Pupils:	A table, a pencil, a stone, basically an inanimate object.
TEACHER:	But is that true? For example, a book grows doesn't it? Sometimes we say, 'the book's growing on me' or it would grow as you write it, wouldn't it?

(They're divided at this point. Some think yes, some no, and some are not sure).

TEACHER:	Let's see if we can agree on some examples. Here's a list to start you off but please add your own examples to it. Grow that list!

Deepening the Learning Pit with questions and activities

When I use the following questions, I let pupils know they should question the questions, and spot assumptions. So, for the question 'What makes people change?', a child might argue that nothing 'makes' them change, they just change. This could develop into an interesting discussion about whether every change has a cause. There would be opportunities for pupils to list possible causes of changes they can identify together.

Questions for young children (3–7):

- Are we growing all the time?
- What does growing mean?
- What does changing mean?
- What makes people change/grow?
- Does everything grow?
- In what ways do people change and grow?
- In what ways do people change but not grow?
- Are there ways in which people grow up but don't change?
- Are there ways in which people neither grow nor change?

Activities

Look at pictures of babies, toddlers, children and adults. Identify examples of change and of growth.

TABLE 8.4

	GROWS	DOESN'T GROW	CHANGES	DOESN'T CHANGE	TYPE OF CHANGE OR GROWTH
The weather					
A river					
A puppy					
An adult					
A child					
An idea					
A dream					
A soap opera					
A computer					
History					
Farming					
A country					
A belief					

Keep a class diary for the week, recording the changes in weather, meals, activities, games, stories and so on, together with the growth of plants.

Read *The very hungry caterpillar* by Eric Carle.

Additional questions for juniors (7–11):

- Does growing always mean changing?
- Does changing always mean growing?
- How many examples can you think of things that grow without changing?
- How many examples can you think of things that change without growing?
- If something increases in size or number, does that mean it has grown?
- Can you grow and not grow at the same time?
- Can you un-grow?
- Will your body always keep growing or changing or both?

Further activities

Link the concepts of change and growth to topics on habitats, evolution, life-cycles, metamorphosis, world development, photosynthesis and so on.

For homework, ask your pupils to find examples at home of things that change, never change, grow, and never grow.

Write a poem with the title, 'Growing and changing'.

Additional questions for adolescents (11–14):

- What are the connections between growth, change and time?
- Is growth a good or bad thing?
- Is change a good or bad thing?
- In what ways can a person's personality grow? Or change?
- How does a person's mind grow?
- Can a person's feelings grow? How?
- Which things do you wish would never change? And never grow?
- Is there anything we can do to alter the way we grow or change?
- When we change our mind, is this really changing?

Additional questions for older pupils (14–18):

- What forms of growth are there?
- Can we stop ourselves changing? Would we want to?
- Can we stop ourselves growing? What would be the benefits?
- Is growth the same as progress?
- In what ways could a person grow without changing?

- In what ways could a person change without developing?
- As people grow, is there anything that remains constant?
- What has changed most in your life?

Stage 3: Construct understanding

Venn diagrams are a useful tool to help pupils identify the key characteristics of concepts such as growth and change.

For 5–7 year olds, ask them to sort a set of objects into two hoops, one representing 'things that grow' and the other 'things that change'.

For older pupils, go for the traditional design of two overlapping hoops, or add a third hoop for 'progress' or 'development'.

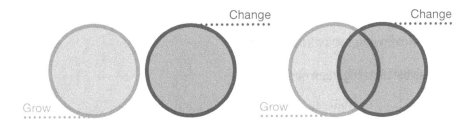

Grow – Change – Grow – Change

Suggested objects for Venn diagram (5–9 years):

carrot	toy	pencil	cup of tea	grandma	seeds
flower	tin of beans	teddy bear	plant	clump of hair	pair of shoes
baby	paper	balloon	water		

Additional concepts for older pupils (9–18):

sadness	happiness	fear	climate	wind	ozone layer
kindness	empathy	love	politicians	old dog	thinking
talents	friendship	personality	traditions	scientific theories	reputations
mind	feelings	families	celebrity	the news	media
teamwork	understanding	culture	art	architecture	construction
faith	beliefs	decisions	school	education	learning
equality	technology	the internet	earth	atmosphere	universe
history	river	tides			

Constructing understanding with secondary pupils (11–18):

Group the following uses of the word 'growth' into as many categories as necessary. Give each category and name and a description.

growth of ideas

product growth

growth of industry

population growth

physical growth (of one's body)

developmental growth

growth of intellect

species growth

growth of genres (TV, internet)

growth in popularity

growth in confidence

growth of self-esteem

Stage 4: Reviewing the learning journey

Possible metacognition questions:

- What's the difference between growth and change?
- Is there anything that doesn't either grow or change with time?
- How many examples have you thought of things that grow without changing?
- How many examples have you thought of things that change without growing?
- Which things do you wish would never change? And never grow?
- How does your idea of growth and change differ from at the beginning of the lesson?
- What questions about growth and change are you left with?

Heroes

Age range 8–18 years

Subjects: English, PSHE, history, media, PE

Stage 1: Identify the concept

'Hero' (from the Greek, *heros*) was originally a word used to describe a person of superhuman powers. This kind of hero is now referred to as a 'superhero' while the term 'hero' is applied to a person who, in the face of danger and adversity or from a position of weakness, displays courage and the will for self-sacrifice – that is, heroism – for some greater good.

Yet the term is also often applied to professional sports stars and other well-known people, perhaps when they display exceptional talents or just because they are successful and admired.

In a work of literature, 'heroes' and 'heroines' are terms used to identify the principal male and female characters. Bad people, such as Macbeth and Lady Macbeth, might be such central characters.

Children and young people will have their heroes but do they associate success with virtue? Can an act that leads to failure still be admired as heroic? Should people be admired mainly for their talents or their virtues (such as bravery)?

Potential for challenge

- Do heroes have to be self-sacrificing?
- Do heroes have to be successful?
- Can someone be a hero if they work for their own gain rather than for the greater good?
- Are heroes always brave?

Stage 2: Problematise the concept

Drawing on ideas from the following dialogue, see if you can unsettle pupils' concept of what a hero is:

TEACHER:	What's a hero?
ADAM:	Someone who's brave.
TEACHER:	Does that mean all brave people are heroes?
ADAM:	I guess.
TEACHER:	But a robber might be brave – does that make him a hero?
RACHEL:	No, heroes have to do good things.
TEACHER:	But wasn't Hitler a hero to many people?
RACHEL:	Yes, I suppose so.
TAS:	Some people still think he's a hero.
TEACHER:	How can Hitler be thought of as a hero?
ANNIE:	Because he was popular.
TEACHER:	Does that mean all popular people are heroes? For example, Britney Spears is popular but she's not a hero, is she?
ANNIE:	No, not really. But she might be a heroine to some people.
TEACHER:	Does that mean only men can be heroes?
ANNIE:	No, heroines are the same thing.
BELINDA:	Anyway, Britney's got too many problems to be a hero or heroine.
TEACHER:	But don't we often hear of cancer-sufferers being heroes and haven't they got loads of problems?
LAURIE:	Yes, but they haven't messed themselves up. Britney has done it to herself.

TEACHER:	Are you suggesting that heroes are faultless, perfect people?
LAURIE:	No, but they don't mess themselves up like Britney has.
TEACHER:	Well what about Gandhi, one of the twentieth century's most respected heroes? He had a troubled relationship with his own children.
ANITA:	I guess everyone has troubles.
TEACHER:	So what makes someone a hero then, if we all have troubles?
KALIM:	A hero does things for other people.
TEACHER:	But in a sense, the cancer sufferer is fighting the disease for their own sake but we still often refer to them as heroes.
ELLIE:	So maybe it's to do with fighting for a just cause.
TEACHER:	Do they have to be successful in that fight?
CHANTELLE:	Yes, otherwise they'd be a failure rather than a success.
TEACHER:	Does that mean the 300 Spartan soldiers who held out for 2 weeks against the might of the Persian army but were ultimately defeated, were not heroes?
KALIM:	No, they were heroes otherwise there wouldn't have been a film about them!
TEACHER:	I don't understand; does that mean losers are heroes?

Deepening the Learning Pit

Further questions to ask juniors (8–11):

- What is a hero?
- Is everyone who is brave a hero?
- Do you have to be brave to be a hero?
- Can someone who is afraid be a hero?
- Can a coward be a hero? (Scooby Doo is sometimes referred to as a cowardly hero)
- Can an animal be a hero?
- Does a hero have to be super-human?
- Do you have to have a super power to be a superhero?

Further activities and questions for adolescents (11–14):

- Do you have to be self-sacrificing to be a hero?
- Can someone who is selfish be a hero?
- Can you still be a hero if no one thinks you are a hero?
- Are famous people always heroes?
- If someone is idolised, does that mean they're a hero?
- Can you perform an act of heroism without being a hero?
- If you perform a heroic act, does that make you a hero?

- Can villains be heroes?
- Could you be a hero just for one day (as sung by David Bowie)?

Analyse and discuss the song, *Holding out for a hero*, sung by Bonnie Tyler, the chorus of which is:

> I need a hero
> I'm holding out for a hero 'til the end of the night
> He's gotta be strong
> And he's gotta be fast
> And he's gotta be fresh from the fight
>
> I need a hero
> I'm holding out for a hero 'til the morning light
> He's gotta be sure
> And it's gotta be soon
> And he's gotta be larger than life

Additional questions for older pupils (14–18):

- Can you be heroic in defeat?
- Does a hero have to be a real person?
- Can a fictional character be a hero?
- Do you have to exist to be a hero?
- Can someone who is evil be a hero?
- Can you be a coward and a hero?
- What is an anti-hero?
- The notion of a 'tragic hero' is one of a good person whose downfall is due to a serious character flaw. However, Macbeth is neither a good man nor does he have simply one fault. So, is he a tragic hero or not? Is he even a hero?
- The term 'feet of clay' is used to describe a hero who has human faults (e.g., Gandhi had a poor relationship with his children). Does every hero have faults?
- Is there such a person as someone with no faults? If so, would they be a hero?

Stage 3: Construct understanding

By comparing the hero with other related concepts, your pupils may gain a clearer insight into the defining characteristics of heroes.

Comparing 'hero' with other concepts (11–18 years)

What are the similarities and differences between the following?

- a hero and a celebrity
- a hero and a villain
- a hero and a superhero
- a hero and an icon
- a hero and a martyr
- a hero and a coward
- a hero and a bully
- a hero and a champion
- a hero and an idol

An alternative way to construct an understanding of heroes is to decide which of these are heroes:

Examples of heroes (11–18 years)

See Table 8.5.

Stage 4: Reviewing the learning journey

Possible metacognition questions:

- Do heroes have to be good people?
- Do heroes have to be successful?
- Are heroes always brave?
- Can someone be a hero if they are selfish?
- Is everyone a hero in their own way?
- How does your idea of heroism differ from at the beginning of the lesson?
- What questions about heroes are you left with?

Identity

Age Range 4 years +

Subjects: PSHE/personal development, citizenship, science, early years

Stage 1: Identify the concept

What makes me 'me'? What are the most important aspects of me: my body, my thoughts, my feelings, my memory, my values? Is my identity most influenced by my genetic make-up, my family, my role in society or what other people think of me? Can I become the person I want to become? Answers to all these questions

TABLE 8.5

EXAMPLE	YES	NO	NOT SURE	REASON
Gandhi				
Winston Churchill				
Florence Nightingale				
Firefighters				
Nelson Mandela				
Your mum				
Your best friend				
Marilyn Manson				
Tiger Woods				
Emmeline Pankhurst				
Batman				
Julius Caesar				
Lady Diana Spencer				
Pablo Picasso				
Jesus				
Mother Teresa				
Osama Bin Laden				
George W Bush				
Jonah Lomu				
Kylie Minogue				
Dick Turpin				
Adolf Hitler				
Al Capone				
Rosa Parks				
Freddie Mercury				
Fidel Castro				
Dalai Lama				
Lassie				

depend on, and influence, the way I create the concept of 'me' and give a sense of unity to my diverse experiences.

These questions have perplexed philosophers for centuries, and children are just as fascinated. In fact, in one sense, the question of identity is the most fundamental question about which children can wonder.

In brief, there are three categories that we might argue make me 'me':

- my self-awareness;
- other people's perception of me;
- my genetics, experiences and personal variations/preferences.

As with 'real', the question of 'me' is one of the few concepts that even very young children (4+) can happily engage with. As they begin to talk about themselves, they soon realise that their own identity is inextricably linked with the identity of others. In other words, how one views oneself is linked to how others view themselves and, in turn, how they view each other.

Perhaps the best starting point is to ask your pupils who they are, how they know who they are and whether who they are stays the same over time.

Stage 2: Problematise the concept

Starting activities for 3–7 years:

1 Give each child a mirror or pass one around the circle. Ask them what they see, followed by:

- How do you know that's you?
- If you were to change your appearance, would you become a different you?

2 Using an interactive whiteboard, import a picture of yourself into a paint programme. Ask the children who they can see and how they know that it is you (they will say 'because it looks like you'). Using the paint programme, change your features, beginning with the colour of your hair, then the size of your ears, then nose, mouth and so on. After each change, ask the group whether or not the picture is still you.

3 Ask the children to each make a poster (or collage) of what makes them 'them'. Encourage them to include pictures of people, animals and objects that are important to them. These could then form the basis for an inquiry into important things – identity and being someone (rather than no one).

Activities for primary children (3–11):

Ask your children to bring in three or four photographs of themselves at different stages of life (e.g., as a baby, a toddler, a reception child and as they are, very recently). Ask them to refer to the pictures when answering the following questions:

- Which one best represents you?
- If they are all you, does that mean looks or appearance are unimportant?
- Presumably you thought different things and had different memories when each of these photographs was taken, so how can they all represent you?
- What things about you have not changed and perhaps will never change?
- Are you a different person when you smile and when you frown?

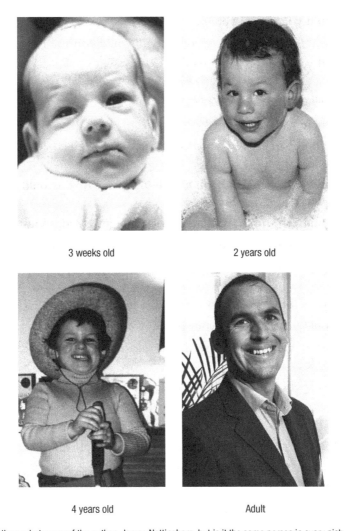

3 weeks old   2 years old

4 years old   Adult

All these photos are of the author, James Nottingham, but is it the same person in every picture?

Deepening the Learning Pit

Further questions for young children (3–7):

■ What makes you 'you'?

■ If you had a different name, would you be a different you?

■ If you looked different, would you still be you?

■ When you play make-believe, are you still you?

■ If you had been born someone else, would you still be you?

■ Are you the same you that you were when you were a baby? (see photos exercise)

■ If you had a bump on the head and suddenly starting saying funny things, would you still be you?

■ If you forgot everything you know, would you still be you?

■ Will you ever be a different you? If so, why?

Additional questions for juniors (7–11):

■ Is there just one of you?

■ Is it possible that a person exactly the same as you could be born with different parents?

■ Is it possible that a person exactly the same as you could be born in another country?

■ Would you still be you if you had different grandparents?

■ Would you still be you if you changed your fingerprints?

■ Would you still be you if everyone in the world thought you were someone else?

■ How is it that you're so sure you're you?

■ Would you like to be your friend?

■ Are you the person you see in the mirror or the person other people see when they look at you?

■ Do experiences make you, change you, or both?

Additional questions for adolescents (11–14):

■ Do you know yourself better than other people know you?

■ Are you a different you in different circumstances?

■ What helps you to be yourself?

■ Would you like to be a different you?

■ If you lost all your memories, would you cease to be you?

- If you were to live as a hermit for the rest of your life, would you become a different you?
- If you swapped brains with someone else, would you still be you?
- Which are you: the person you were, the person you are, or the person you will be?
- If you had different beliefs or opinions, would you be a different person?

Further questions to ask older pupils (14–18):

- If everyone in the world mistook you for someone else, who would you be?
- Which part of you has remained constant throughout your life?
- Which bit of you do you suppose will never change?
- If you were to witness an atrocity, would you still be the same person afterwards?
- Do you think everyone who gets caught up in war becomes a different person?
- If you read a so-called 'life-changing' book, do you think you'd become a different you?
- Do you suppose people go through counselling to improve themselves or to change themselves completely? Why?

Stage 3: Construct understanding

The following exercise should help pupils to piece together a characterisation of what makes them 'them'.

Who are you? (an activity for 9–16 years)

See Table 8.6 overleaf.

Stage 4: Reviewing the learning journey

Possible metacognition questions:

- What makes you 'you'?
- How do you know that this makes you 'you'?
- Is it true there is only one of you? Explain.
- Will you always be you?
- How many different identities will you have in your lifetime?
- How does your idea of identity differ from at the beginning of the lesson?
- What questions about identity are you left with?

TABLE 8.6

ARE YOU . . .	YES	NO	NOT SURE	REASON
your body?				
all the things you've done in life?				
your mind?				
your personality?				
the sum of all your feelings?				
who your family think you are?				
who your best friend thinks you are?				
who God thinks you are?				
who you think you are?				
the person you always were?				
the person you'll always be?				

Knowledge

Age range 8–16

Subjects: All

Although knowledge is a concept that appears in all subjects, the examples we would consider differ from subject to subject (e.g. scientific knowledge, artistic knowledge and human knowledge all seem to have different qualities). This lesson plan takes a generic approach which can be used across the curriculum. It considers what it means to know, how this is different from understanding, and whether the knowing of something and someone is the same kind of thing.

In the tradition of Western thought, there is no such thing as wrong knowledge. Either it is true, in which case it is knowledge, or it is not true, in which case it is not knowledge. Indeed, to prefix knowledge with 'true' is like using the prefix 'sweet' with sugar (there is no knowledge that is not true in the same way that there is no sugar that is not sweet). Some Eastern philosophies have different approaches to truth, with more emphasis on enlightenment through experience and reflection.

Stage 1: Identify the concept

'Knowing' seems to involve being sure of a truth or being sure that something you are aware of is true. For example, I know that gravity exists. In contrast, 'understand' tends to mean that we grasp the relationships between the conditions that produced it and the effects that flow from it. For example, I know that gravity exists, whereas scientists might say they understand gravity because they understand how it is created and what impact it has on us.

Complexities of the concept

The complexities that this lesson plan is designed to tease out include:

- the difference between knowing and knowledge;
- how knowing something and knowing someone seem to be different;
- how personal knowledge and general or global knowledge might differ (more correctly referred to as subjective and objective);
- whether you can understand something without having knowledge about it;
- whether you know something without knowing that you know.

Stage 2: Problematise the concept

Drawing on ideas from the following dialogue, see if you can unsettle pupils' concept of what knowledge is:

TEACHER:	What does knowledge mean?
ADAM:	It's about knowing things.
TEACHER:	I know your name. Does that mean I have knowledge about you?
ADAM:	Yes.
TEACHER:	But do I know you in the same way that your mum knows you?
RACHEL:	No, that's different.
TEACHER:	How is it different?
RACHEL:	Adam's mum knows him really well. You only know him a bit.
TEACHER:	Which bit?
ADAM:	You know what she means. My mum knows me really well. She's known me a lot longer than you have.
TEACHER:	Does that mean the longer you know someone or something, the more knowledge you have about them? I've known my teeth ever since they grew in my mouth. Does that mean I know my teeth really well?
TAS:	I guess so.
TEACHER:	But do you think I know my teeth better than my dentist knows them?
TAS:	Of course not. Your dentist is an expert on teeth, including yours.
TEACHER:	But my dentist hasn't known my teeth as long as I have. In fact, I changed dentists about 2 years ago. So, do you think this new dentist still knows my teeth?
ANITA:	Yes, but that's different. She knows about teeth and so when she looks at your teeth, she understands more than you do.
TEACHER:	What do you mean?
ANITA:	Well, your dentist has studied teeth. She knows the names of all the teeth, what they're for and what they should look like.
TEACHER:	So, she has knowledge about my teeth in the sense that she knows lots of facts about teeth? She knows the facts about teeth.
KALIM:	Exactly.
TEACHER:	So, if I know the names of all the planets in our solar system, does that mean I know those planets?
ELLIE:	No, it means you have knowledge about them but it doesn't mean you know them.
TEACHER:	But how can that be? I thought we said at the beginning that knowledge is about knowing things?
SAM:	Well, it is about knowing things. It's about knowing the facts. For example, I know that the world is round.
TEACHER:	That's a very interesting idea because people used to 'know' that the world was flat. So what can we say about their knowledge?
FRANCES:	They were wrong. Their knowledge was wrong.
TEACHER:	But I thought we said that knowledge is what we know to be right. So how can knowledge be wrong?
PAUL:	Knowledge is whatever you think is right at the time.
MOHAMMED:	But if I think I can fly, that doesn't mean that's right, does it?

PAUL:	No, it means you're deluded.
TEACHER:	Does that mean that when our ancestors knew the world was flat, they were deluded?
SUSAN:	Where does that leave us? What is knowledge?

Deepening the Learning Pit

How do we know that . . .

- £1 is worth the same as 100p?
- € 2 + € 2 = € 4?
- we know something?
- fire burns (things)?
- if we fall over, it hurts?
- the earth is round?
- we are made up of DNA?
- the ancient Egyptians built the pyramids?

What's the difference between:

- knowing Paris is the capital of France and knowing Paris?
- knowing your address and knowing the house you live in?
- knowing something and knowing someone?
- the knowledge your dentist has about your teeth and the knowledge you have about your teeth?
- knowing how to cook an egg and knowing that eggs come from chickens?

Who knows?

- Can you have the same knowledge about something as someone else does?
- Can you know what another person knows?
- If I have toothache, can you know how it feels?
- What do you think a dog knows?
- Do you think a dog knows he knows these things?
- Is it possible that people don't really know anything?

Further questions

1   Can I have knowledge of something and yet not know it? (e.g. I know about various cities in the world though I cannot say I know them all).

2   Is it possible to understand something without having knowledge about it? (e.g. I might say I understand how someone feels when their pet dies even though I've never had a pet).

3   What did Albert Einstein mean when he said: 'Whoever undertakes to set himself up as a judge of Truth and Knowledge is shipwrecked by the laughter of the gods'?

4   Can knowledge change? (e.g. we once knew the world was flat, now we know the world is round; or, we knew the sun rotated around the earth, now we know it is the other way round).

NB Your pupils might enjoy knowing that there is an active Flat Earth Society, whose members claim, among other things, that the Apollo moon landing was a hoax and that footage was in fact a sci-fi film made by Arthur C. Clarke. For more details, visit: www.theflatearthsociety.org.

The cow in the field

Ask your pupils to discuss the following scenario and decide whether Farmer Field 'knew' his cow, Daisy, was in the field.

Farmer Field is concerned about his prize cow, Daisy. In fact, he is so concerned that when his dairyman tells him that Daisy is in the field, happily grazing, he says he needs to know for certain. He doesn't want to have a 99 per cent probability that Daisy is safe, he wants to be able to say he knows Daisy is safe.

Farmer Field goes to the field and, standing by the gate, sees in the distance, behind some trees, a white and black shape that he recognises as his favourite cow. He goes back to the dairy and tells his friend that he knows Daisy is in the field. Yet, at this point, does Farmer Field really know this is the case?

The dairyman says he will check too, and goes to the field. There he finds Daisy having a nap in a hollow, behind a bush, well out of sight of the gate. He also spots a large piece of black and white paper that has got caught in a tree. Daisy is in the field, as Farmer Field thought. But was he right to say that he knew she was?

The philosopher, Martin Cohen, who described this scenario originally,[87] says that in this case the farmer:

- believed the cow was safe;
- had evidence that this was so (his belief was justified);
- knew that his cow was safe (i.e. it was true).

However, we might still feel that the farmer did not really know it. Herein lies the core of the problem of 'knowledge as justified true belief'.

Stage 3: Construct understanding

Making comparisons may help pupils to decide whether knowledge is different from or similar to other concepts such as fact, belief and experience.

What are the similarities and differences between the following?

- knowing and guessing
- knowing and believing
- knowing and thinking
- my knowledge and general knowledge
- my knowledge and facts
- knowledge and experience
- knowledge and wisdom
- knowledge and data
- knowledge and evidence
- knowledge and truth
- knowledge and proof

Which of the following statements in Table 8.7 (overleaf) count as knowledge?

Stage 4: Reviewing the learning journey

Possible metacognition questions:

- Does knowledge come from knowing something?
- Can you know something without having knowledge about it?
- Do we ever really know anything?
- Can you know something without knowing that you know?
- Do you need to believe something to know it?
- How does your idea of knowledge differ from at the beginning of the lesson?
- What questions about knowledge are you left with?

Proof and evidence

Age range 9–18

Subjects: All

Stage 1: Identify the concept

It is notoriously difficult to prove anything beyond all doubt. For example, a pupil might say they can prove who they are by showing their passport, but this might be a forgery. Or they might say they can prove that the sun will rise every morning but there is a minute possibility that the world will end before tomorrow and with it all sunrises! This may seem facetious but it is actually a rich vein of thought to explore with pupils. You can have a lot of fun, and pupils will gain a greater insight into the problems of proof and evidence.

TABLE 8.7

	YES	NO	NOT SURE	REASON
The earth is round.				
Lima is the capital city of Peru.				
It is against the law to drink and drive.				
At the end of the 07–08 season, Manchester United were the best football team in Europe.				
Today, team X (whoever is top of the league) are the best team in this country.				
It is wrong to kill.				
We have found no signs of alien life.				

Complexities of the concept

- What is the difference between proof and evidence?
- Is it possible to prove anything at all?
- In what circumstances might enough evidence prove a case?
- What is enough evidence?

Stage 2: Problematise the concept

Drawing on ideas from the following dialogue, see if you can unsettle pupils' concept of what proof and evidence is:

TEACHER:	I bet you cannot prove anything to me!
ADAM:	I can! I can prove that I'm sitting here.
TEACHER:	How?
ADAM:	Well, look, here I am! (waving)
TEACHER:	But how do I know that I'm not just imagining you?
RACHEL:	You could walk over and touch Adam.
TEACHER:	But when I touch things in dreams, it doesn't mean I've actually touched them – so perhaps I'm dreaming this whole conversation.
RACHEL:	But you need to be asleep to dream and you're not asleep.
TAS:	No, you don't, you can daydream without being asleep.
TEACHER:	Good point, Tas. So can anyone prove that this isn't all a dream?
ANNIE:	You don't smell things in your dreams but I can smell things here.
TEACHER:	But how do you know people can't smell in their dreams?
ANNIE:	Well, I never have.
TEACHER:	Is that enough evidence to prove that people can't smell?
LAURIE:	I guess not.
TEACHER:	OK, let's take an example. Could we ever prove that ghosts do or do not exist?
ANITA:	Yes, if someone was to see a ghost that would prove ghosts exist.
TEACHER:	But what if no one else could see this ghost?
ANITA:	OK, if everyone could see the ghost that would prove the existence of ghosts.
TEACHER:	Does that mean that if just one person cannot see the ghost, then there are no ghosts?
KALIM:	No, if the majority of people can see the ghost, then that would be enough.
TEACHER:	So is proof to do with what the majority believe?
ELLIE:	Yes.
TEACHER:	But there was a period of history, in the tenth century, when the majority of people thought the world was flat – so had they proved the world was flat?

Deepening the Learning Pit

Activities and questions for 9–13 years:

1   Ask your pupils to pair up. Pupil A should come up with an example of something they can prove; pupil B should try to find a way to call into question the absolute certainty of pupil A's assertion.

2   Ask groups of pupils to come up with as long a list as possible of things they can prove. In each case, encourage them to find exceptions that cast doubt upon their assertions.

Questions

Use the following questions to think about different aspects of proof and evidence. In each case, encourage the pupils to find exceptions that cast doubt upon the assertion.

■   If we can touch, taste, smell, hear and see something, is that enough evidence to prove something exists?

■   If our gut instinct tells us something is real, does this prove its existence?

■   If my pet is a bird, is that enough to prove that my pet can fly?

■   If I have a pet dog, does that prove my pet can bark?

■   Do you have enough evidence to prove beyond all doubt who you are?

■   If no counter-evidence can be found, does that mean something has been proved?

■   It's the beginning of December and Tom the Turkey is reflecting on his life. Every day for the past 300 days, Tom has been cared for by Farmer Jones. He's been well fed, watered, sheltered and given medicines whenever he needed them. Is this enough evidence to prove that Farmer Jones loves Tom?

■   The sun has risen every day since the earth was formed. Is this enough evidence to prove that the sun will rise tomorrow?

■   If your fingerprints were found at the scene of a crime, does that prove you were there?

■   You see smoke – is that evidence or proof (or neither) that there is a fire?

Additional questions and activities for older pupils (14–18):

Ask the pupils whether they think Descartes was right in the following extract:

> The philosopher, Descartes, is renowned for subjecting everything to doubt and, in so doing, questioning whether anything can ever be proved. A classic example of this is whether we can prove that life is not a dream. In the end, he decided that there was just one thing he could prove: that he was something.

He went on to claim that even in mathematics nothing could be proved since there was a tiny possibility that a malicious demon was trying to deceive him at all times. His well-known claim, 'I think, therefore I am', was the only thing he felt he could prove because even if a malicious demon were trying to trick him, the demon would be unable to trick him into thinking he didn't exist (because to doubt one's existence is to exist as a doubting thing).

Use the following questions to extend thoughts further. As with younger pupils, encourage everyone to think of exceptions that will cast doubt on the certainty of proof.

- There has never been an occurrence of someone living forever. Does that prove that one day I too will die?
- Does evidence need to be incontrovertible to prove something?
- If one has absolute proof for the repeated occurrence of an event, is that enough to predict with absolute certainty that it will happen in the future?
- How could you prove to a blind person that there are colours?
- The philosopher, David Hume, wrote, 'A wise man proportions his belief to the evidence'. What did he mean by this?
- Has anything ever been proved for all time?
- How much evidence is required to prove something?
- Can you prove that you are not simply a figment of someone's imagination?
- If you are able to prove something which is later found to be false, was it ever proved?
- Do we really need proof?

Stage 3: Construct understanding

Encouraging your pupils to draw comparisons between similar or linked concepts may help them to focus on the important characteristics of proof and evidence. What are the similarities and differences between the following?

- proof and evidence
- evidence and data
- proof and facts
- proof and truth
- proof and knowledge
- proof and faith
- proof and observation
- evidence and facts

Stage 4: Reviewing the learning journey

Possible metacognition questions:

- Is proof the same as evidence?
- How much evidence do we need to prove something?
- Is it possible to prove anything without hindsight?
- Why is it important to search for evidence and proof?
- What are the problems with evidence and proof?
- How do your ideas of proof and evidence differ from at the beginning of the lesson?
- What questions about proof and evidence are you left with?

Reality

Age range 4 years +

Subjects: All

Stage 1: Identify the concept

The concept 'real' is not at all clear, which is perhaps partly why it holds such fascination for children and adults alike. One of just a handful of concepts that children as young as 4 can happily discuss, it is likely to come up with pupils of all ages and within many areas of the curriculum.

Some philosophers have said that all our experience (including sleeping) is a different 'reality' from the reality of the physical world which exists independently of human experience. That said, this is not globally accepted nor is it particularly a view that we should encourage with children. However, what is clear is that we ought to be able to establish criteria for distinguishing between appearance and reality. Though children need to fantasise, imagine and dream, they also need an understanding that these activities might not be 'real'.

One way of exploring the concept is to look at different ways in which something can be unreal, for example, a plastic banana, a dream, monopoly money, magic and stories. Though they are, arguably, all unreal (or fake) they seem to be unreal in different ways. And that is without bringing in such things as optical illusions that seem to be one thing despite being another, for example, train tracks that seem to converge in the distance, or 'magic' mirrors at fairs.

Complexities of the concept

- How do we know whether something is real or not?
- In what ways are toys real?

■ Is there anything real about reality TV, since it is most often deliberately set up to provoke certain behaviours or situations?

■ How do we know that life is real?

Stage 2: Problematise the concept

This is a favourite of mine to introduce with 4 and 5 year olds, although it can easily be adapted for older pupils. A guide to the questioning techniques I use can be found on page 59 of the Challenge chapter.

I place in front of the children a juicy red apple and a plastic apple and begin with 'What do you see here?'

CHILDREN:	Two apples.
ME:	Are they the same?
CHILDREN:	No, one's real and the other is plastic.
ME:	Does that mean the plastic one is not real?
CHILDREN:	Yes.
ME:	But does that mean everything that is plastic is not real, for example, this chair? This chair is plastic so does that mean it's not real?
CHILDREN:	No!
YES:	Then why is this plastic apple not real?
CHILDREN:	It is real.
ME:	So they're both real, is that right?
CHILDREN:	Yes.
ME:	So, what about the other apple? (pointing to an invisible apple) Is that real?
CHILDREN:	No!
ME:	Why not?
CHILDREN:	Because we can't see it.
ME:	But we can't see your teacher at the moment, can we? Let's look around the room, can anyone see her?
CHILDREN:	No.
ME:	Does that mean Mrs Brown is not real?
CHILDREN:	Of course not.
ME:	So why do you think my third, juicy red apple isn't real?
CHILDREN:	Because we've never seen your apple but we've seen Mrs Brown lots of times.
ME:	So, if you've never seen something, does that mean it's not real?
CHILDREN:	Yes.
ME:	But none of you have ever seen my dog, Hector, and he's real, isn't he?

This is where opinion becomes divided and we talk about evidence, believability and trust.

Deepening the Learning Pit

Questions to ask young children (3–7):

- When we dress up, are we real?
- Are your dreams real?
- Are toys real? What about toy cars or plastic animals?
- Are things that we can't see, real?
- How do you know if something is real or not real?
- Is television real?

NB AVOID reference to the reality (or otherwise) of Santa and the Tooth Fairy!

Additional questions for juniors (7–11):

- What's the difference between being real and being alive?
- When you look in the mirror, is your reflection real?
- Do you need to be able see, touch, feel, smell or taste something to know it's real?
- When are stories real?
- Is what's real for you the same as what's real for your friends?
- Is the sky real?

Additional questions for adolescents (11–14):

- Can something be real and not real at the same time?
- What's the difference between reality and perception?
- How do you decide when to believe what you see?
- What are the connections between reality, truth and fact?
- Can something that doesn't exist be real?
- Are people who have died still real?

Further questions to ask older pupils (14–18):

- What is the difference between reality and virtual reality?
- What is real about reality TV?
- Does one enter a different reality in one's dreams?
- If something has not happened yet but is inevitable, is it real?
- What did Albert Einstein mean when he said: 'Reality is merely an illusion, albeit a very persistent one'?

Stage 3: Construct understanding

The following activities should help your pupils begin to form a clearer idea of what 'real' and reality are:

Young children (3–7):

See Table 8.8 overleaf.

Venn diagram

Sort a set of objects into two hoops, one representing 'real' and the other 'not real'. Keep the hoops separate to begin with and then progress to overlapping hoops, perhaps changing the labels to 'real' and 'pretend' (can things be real and pretend at the same time?)

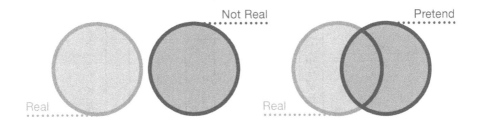

Also consider the following questions:

- What's the difference between a real fireman or nurse and when we dress up as a fireman/nurse?
- What's the difference between imaginary play and physical play?
- Is all play 'pretend'? If so, does that mean play is not real?
- What's the difference between dressing up (e.g. as a monster) and getting dressed?
- If dressing up is 'pretend' then are you not real when you dress up?

Additional activities for juniors (7–11):

Place these words and concepts along a continuum between 'real' and 'not real', see page 181.

TABLE 8.8

	REAL	NOT REAL	NOT SURE	REASON
Plastic food				
Dreams				
Stories				
Monopoly money				
The Gruffalo*				
Spiderman				
Heroes				

*The Gruffalo refers to a character in a picture book (Donaldson, J. and Scheffler, A., *The Gruffalo*, Macmillan Children's Books, 1999). However, you could use any character well known to your pupils.

REAL   NOT REAL

Role play	Pretend	Forgery	Dressing up
Fictional character	Monsters	Toy soldier	Teddy bear
Doll	The sky	A dream	Thoughts
Rules	Words	Emotions	Television
The news	Shadows		

Concentric circles: Real

In your group, decide where these words fit in the concentric circles diagram:

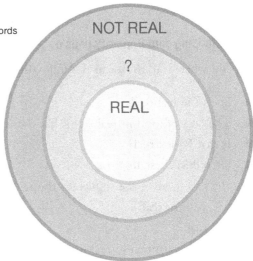

Concentric circles: Real

In your group, decide where these words fit in the concentric circles diagram:

- Fake
- Authentic
- Pretend
- Good
- Bogus
- Genuine
- Realistic
- False
- Bona fide
- Counterfeit
- Copy
- Mock-up

Additional comparisons for older pupils (11–18):

Pick five of these concept pairs. Describe the similarities and differences between the two concepts in each case.

- real and not real
- reality and truth
- fact and fiction
- real and imaginary
- reality and feeling
- reality TV and TV news
- real and dead
- real and supernatural
- reality and perception
- real and make-believe
- real and pretend
- real and tangible
- reality and virtual reality
- real and alive
- real and copy
- authentic and real

Understanding contemporary uses of 'real'

Explain what 'real' means in the following examples:

- She's the real deal.
- The cost of food in real terms has risen by 15 per cent.
- Is that Rolex real?
- He sells real estate.
- She's so in love, she thinks it's the real thing.
- Are you for real?
- Get real!
- We saw it happen in real time.

Stage 4: Reviewing the learning journey

Possible metacognition questions:

- How can we tell if something is real or not?

- Can something be real and not real (or fake) at the same time?
- Are toys real?
- How can we be sure that our lives are real?
- Is the future real?
- How does your idea of reality differ from at the beginning of the lesson?
- What questions about real are you left with?

Shape

Age range 4 years +

Subjects: Art, design & technology, maths

Stage 1: Identify the concept

Shape is a fascinating concept. Young children enjoy talking about shapes because they are central to their ongoing exploration of the world around them. Older children become very interested when we begin to ask questions such as 'does everything have a shape?' or 'do ideas have shapes?' (if not, then what does the phrase 'our ideas are starting to take shape' mean?)

Key distinctions to bear in mind when challenging pupils about shape are:

- Shape is formed when lines meet. Shapes are always 2D. Some shapes are geometric (circle, rectangle, triangle) and some are organic or irregular.
- Forms are 3D. They have height, width and thickness. Common forms include spheres, cubes, cylinders, cones and pyramids.

Complexities of the concept

- Does everything have a shape?
- Do abstract notions such as ideas have shape?
- Can smells, tastes or sounds have shape?
- Is there really such a thing as the 'perfect shape'?

Stage 2: Problematise the concept

The following dialogue with 9-year-olds gives some ideas as to how children's notion of shape might be challenged:

TEACHER: How many shapes can you see in the room?

(The children begin to name shapes)

TEACHER:	Does everything have a shape?
CHILDREN:	Yes.
TEACHER:	So what shape is this book?
CHILDREN:	Square.
TEACHER:	And what about this apple?
CHILDREN:	Round (or circle).
TEACHER:	What about this hoop?
CHILDREN:	Round (or circle).
TEACHER:	But the hoop and the apple look very different to me, so how can they have the same shape?

(Various answers)

TEACHER: So some shapes of the same name can look different to each other – how strange! Let's see if the same can be said of rectangles.

Gather together a set of different sized/shaped rectangles

TEACHER:	What do they have in common?
CHILDREN:	They all have four sides.
TEACHER:	But so do squares, don't they?
CHILDREN:	Yes, but rectangles have sides with different lengths.
TEACHER:	So, this shape is a rectangle because it has different length sides? (showing a right-angled triangle)
CHILDREN:	No! Rectangles have all got four sides.
TEACHER:	Ah, OK. Like this then:

CHILDREN:	No. They have to have two lots of two lines of the same length.
TEACHER:	Like this?

CHILDREN: No, that's a bow tie. The lines are not allowed to cross on a rectangle.
TEACHER: So, this is not a rectangle then?

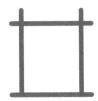

Many opinions are shared at this point!

Deepening the Learning Pit

Questions to ask young children (3–7):

■   How many shapes can you see right now?

■   Do you have a favourite shape? Why?

■   Is every shape like the one you're describing, your favourite?

■   Does everything have a shape?

■   What shape is a teddy bear?

■   What shape are you?

■   What shape are your dreams?

■   Do sounds have shapes?

■   When you look at a circle, how do you know it's a circle? (for 6 and 7 year olds)

Additional questions for pupils aged 8–14:

■   What is a shape?

■   Does every shape have a name?

■   If we all look at this shape, are we all seeing the same shape?

■   Could things be the same shape but a different size?

■   Could things be the same size but a different shape?

■   What shape would the colour red be?

■   What shape is the sound of a police siren?

■   What shape is the smell of coffee?

■   Does the taste of lemon have a shape?

■   Do feelings have shape? For example, happiness or sadness?

■ Do ideas have shapes?

■ What do we mean when we say 'his idea was beginning to take shape'?

■ What shape are your dreams?

Further questions to ask older pupils (14–18):

■ Is there such a thing as the perfect shape?

■ Can you imagine the perfect shape?

■ Does the perfect shape exist only in our minds?

■ Is a cube a square? What are the similarities and differences?

■ What's the difference between looking like a cube and being a cube?

■ What does the phrase 'the shape of things to come' mean?

■ What is meant by 'shape up or ship out'?

■ Are there an infinite number of shapes in the same way as there are an infinite number of numbers?

■ If two things were of the same shape but different size, would that make one a model of the other?

Stage 3: Construct understanding

The following activities should help your pupils to begin constructing a conceptualisation of shape.

Suggested activities (3–7):

1   Group objects into different categories of shapes. For example, begin with shapes that have curves, and shapes that only have straight lines. Then progress onto shapes that have agreed names, and shapes that don't (organic shapes).

2   Count the number of different shapes the children can see in the classroom.

3   Look at photographs together and ask the children to name all the different shapes they can see.

4   Ask the children to each draw ten different shapes and then place them into three categories.

Additional activities (8–14 years):

1   Shapes in the alphabet (see 'alphabet shapes' activities shown below).

2   Work out how many shapes can be made from four, five and six cubes.

3   Predict the number of shapes that could be made from seven, eight and nine cubes.

4   Find as many examples of organic shapes as possible then create names for them.

5 In pairs, one pupil describes a shape (without naming it) for the other one to draw.

Alphabet shapes

Here is a set of letters. What do they have in common?

J C U

Here is the same set, with another letter added. Now what features do they share?

J C U S

Here's another set. Say what is different about the shape of these compared to the first set.

H M W K

Here are two different ways to write the letter, 'J'. How would this difference affect the set it belonged to?

J J

Create four sets of letters, each with different properties. Ask your friend to guess which properties you used in each case. Here's one to start you off.

D P B

Discussion time

- The letter X seems to be different to all the other letters. Why?
- Which are the most artistically pleasing letters?
- Which letters do you like writing most and why?
- Which are the three best letters and why?
- If you wrote all the letters in lower case, how would this change their properties?
- Here are some letters used in other languages. What do you think of them?

  Å Ø Ê Æ Ω Œ Δ И

Stage 4: Reviewing the learning journey

Possible metacognition questions:

- What are shapes?

- Why are shapes important?
- Does everything have a shape?
- Do abstract notions such as ideas, thoughts, smells or tastes have shape?
- Does the perfect shape exist?
- How does your idea of shape differ from at the beginning of the lesson?
- What questions about shape are you left with?

Here endeth the lessons

Notes

'The secret to creativity is knowing how to hide your sources.'

(Einstein, 1979–1955)

Preface

1   SAPERE, Society for Advancing Philosophical Enquiry and Reflection in Education, UK., www.sapere.org.uk.

Chapter 1: What is challenging learning?

2   Lipman, M., *Thinking in education*, (1st edn), Cambridge University Press, 1991.

3   Hattie, J., 'Influences on student learning', Inaugural Lecture: Professor of Education, University of Auckland, August 1999.

4   Lipman, M., 1991.

5   Einstein, A., *Out of my later years*, Thames and Hudson, 1950.

6   Hattie, J., 1999.

7   RAIS, Raising Aspirations In Society, UK. www.sustained-success. com/index.php/899.

Chapter 2: Feedback

8   See www.dylanwiliamcenter.com/is-the-feedback-you-are-giving-students-helping-or-hindering.

9   Winne, P. H. and Butler, D. L., 'Student cognition in learning from teaching', in Husen, T. and Postlewaite, T. (eds), *International encyclopaedia of education*, (2nd edn), Oxford, UK, 1994, pp. 5738–45.

10   Lysakowski, R. S. and Walberg, H. J., 'Instructional effects of cues, participation and corrective feedback: a quantitative synthesis', *American Educational Research Journal*, Winter 1982, Vol. 19, No. 4, pp. 559–78.

11   Marzano, R. J., Pickering, D. J. and Pollock, J. E., *Classroom instruction that works: research-based strategies for increasing student achievement*, ASCD Publications, 2001.

12   Black, P. and Wiliam, D., *Working inside the black box*, King's College, London, 2002.

13   Hattie, J., 1999.

14   Lysakowski, R. S. and Walberg, H. J., 1982.

15   Hattie, J., *Visible learning: a synthesis of over 800 meta-analyses relating to achievement*, Routledge, 2009.

16   'Assessment for Learning: beyond the black box', Assessment Reform Group, QCA website (www.qca.org.uk/libraryAssets/media/beyond_black_box2.pdf).

17   Dweck, C. S., *Self-theories: their role in motivation, personality and development*, Taylor & Francis, 2000.

18   Black, P. and Wiliam, D., *Inside the black box*, King's College, London, 1998.

19   Hattie, J. and Timperley, H., 'The power of feedback', *American Educational Research Journal*, March 2007, Vol. 77, No. 1, pp. 81–112.

20   Nuthall, G. A., 'The cultural myths and realities of classroom teaching and learning: a personal journey'. *Teachers College Record*, 2005, Vol. 107, No. 5, pp. 895–934.

21   Hattie, J. and Timperley, H., 2007.

22   Dinkmeyer, D. and Dreikurs, R., *Encouraging children to learn*, Brunner-Routledge, 2000.

23   Williams, S. and Wegerif, R., *Radical encouragement: creating cultures for learning*, Imaginative Minds, 2006.

24   The Community of Inquiry is a term particularly associated with Philosophy for Children and is adapted from a notion introduced by the philosopher, Charles Sanders Peirce. See Lipman, 1991, and Charles Sanders Peirce, 'The fixation of belief' in *Philosophical writings of Peirce*, edited by Justus Buchler, Dover Publications, New York, 1955.

25   See www.p4c.com for a brief history of Philosophy for Children.

26   This section was written by Steve Williams for the website, www.p4c.com, an enterprise set up by Steve, myself and Roger Sutcliffe to provide resources for teachers doing Philosophy for Children.

27   See for example www.p4c.com: An international resource and collaboration service for P4C; www.icpic.org: The International Council of Philosophical Inquiry with Children (ICPIC); www.sapere. org.uk: Home of SAPERE, the charity that supports P4C training and accreditation in the UK.

28   Hattie, J., 2009.

29   Marzano, R. J., Pickering, D. J. and Pollock, J. E., 2001.

30   Black, P. and Wiliam, D., 1998.

31   Butler, R., 'Task-involving and ego-involving properties of evaluation: effects of different psychology feedback conditions on motivational perceptions, interest, and performance', *Journal of Educational Psychology*, 1997, Vol. 79, No. 4, pp. 474–82.

32   See Hattie, J., 2009.

33   Rowe, M. B., 'Wait time: slowing down may be a way of speeding up!', *Journal of Teacher Education*, 1986, Vol. 37, No. 1.

34   Sadler, D. R., 'Formative assessment and the design of instructional systems', *Instructional Science*, 1989, Vol. 18, pp. 121–2.

35   Dweck, C. S., *Mindset*, Random House, 2006.

36   Greene, B. A. and Miller, R. B., 'Influences on achievement: goals, perceived ability and cognitive engagement', *Contemporary Educational Psychology*, 1996, Vol. 21.

37   Hattie, J., 2009.

38   Dweck, C. S., 2000.

39   Marzano *et al.*, 2001.

40   Black, P. and Wiliam, D., 2002.

41   Black, P. and Wiliam, D., 2002.

Chapter 3: Application

42   Wigfield, A. L. and Eccles, J. S., 'Expectancy-value theory of achievement motivation', *Contemporary Educational Psychology*, 2000, Vol. 25, pp. 68–81.

43   Wigfield, A. L. and Eccles, J. S., 2000.

44   From 'The man who invented management: Why Peter Drucker's ideas still matter' *Business Week*, 28th November 2008.

45   See www.habits-of-mind.net.

46   See www.buildinglearningpower.co.uk.

47   Hattie, J., 2009, p. 47.

48   Dweck, C. S., 2000.

49   Dweck, C. S., 2006.

50   From www.carlrogers.info.

51   Dweck, C. S., 2000.

52   Nicholls, J. G. and Miller, A. T., 'The differentiation of the concepts of difficulty and ability', *Child Development*, 1984, pp. 951–9.

53   Hattie, J., 2009.

54   Hattie, J., 2009.

55   Dweck, C. S., 2006.

Chapter 4: Challenge

56   Lipman, M., 1991.

57   Rosenthal, R. and Jacobson, L., *Pygmalion in the classroom: teacher expectation and pupils' intellectual development*, Holt, Rinehart & Winston, New York, 1968.

58   Bruner, J. S., *The culture of education*, Harvard University Press, Cambridge, MA, 1996.

59   Vygotsky, L. S., *Mind and society: the development of higher mental processes*, Harvard University Press, Cambridge, MA, 1978.

60   Bloom, B., *Taxonomy of educational objectives: the classification of educational goals*, Susan Fauer Company, 1956, pp. 201–7.

61   Rowe, M. B., 1986.

62   Lipman, M., *Thinking in education*, (2nd edn), Cambridge University Press, 2003.

63   Lipman, M. and Sharp, A., *Wondering at the world, the manual for 'Kio and Gus'*, ICPIC, 1986.

64   Rowe, M. B., 1986.

Chapter 5: Thinking

65   Einstein, A., *Out of my later years*, Thames and Hudson, 1950.

66   Lipman, M. and Sharp, A., 1986.

67   Bloom, B., 1956.

68   Dolya, G., *Vygotsky in action in the early years*, Routledge, 2007.

69   From GCSE History B (Modern World) Paper 1 (Core Content with The USA, 1919 – 1941) published by OCR and sat by pupils on Tuesday 3rd June 2008. Photograph is copyright of Corbis (www.corbis.com).

70   See www.edwdebono.com/debono/po.htm.

71   Critical, Creative and Caring thinking are dimensions of thinking emphasised first in the work of Matthew Lipman. See Lipman, M., 1991.

72   Rogers, C. R. and Roethlisberger, F. J. 'Barriers and gateways to communication', *Harvard Business Review*, July/August 1952.

73   Bloom, B., 1956.

Chapter 6: Self-esteem

74   Rosenberg, M., *Society and the adolescent self-image*, Princeton University Press, 1965.

75   Bandura, A., *Self-efficacy: the exercise of control*, Freeman, New York, 1997, p. 604.

76   Maslow, A. H., 'A theory of human motivation', originally published in *Psychological Review*, 1943, Vol. 50, No.4, pp. 370–96.

77   Dweck, C. S., *Self-theories: their role in motivation, personality and development*, Taylor & Francis, 2000.

78   Dweck, C. S., 2000.

79   Dweck, C. S., 2000.

80   See Ginott, H. G., *Between parent and child*, (2nd edn), Crown Publications, 2004.

Chapter 7: The Learning Pit

81   See: www.edwdebono.com.

82   Dale, E., *Audio-visual methods in teaching*, revised edition, Henry Holt and Company, New York, 1954.

83   Newell, A., *Unified theories of cognition*, Harvard University Press, 1991.

84   Chi, A. and van Lehn, K., 'A model of the self-explanation effect', *Journal of the Learning Sciences*, January 1992, Vol. 2, No. 1, January 1992.

Chapter 8: Lesson ideas

85   Lipman, M., 2003.

86   Hattie, J., 1999.

87   Cohen, M., *101 philosophy problems*, Routledge, 1999.

Index